INSIGHTS

The Healing Paths
of the
Radical Spiritualist

ROBERT EGBY

Author of the Award Winning

The Quest of the Radical Spiritualist

INSIGHTS

The Healing Paths
of the
Radical Spiritualist

ROBERT EGBY

Three Mile Point Publishing

Chaumont, NY

Published by:
Three Mile Point Publishing
26941 Three Mile Point Road
Chaumont, NY 13622
www.threemilepointpublishing.com
Phone: 315-654-2060

Book formatting and cover design by: Kimberly Martin

First published:
Three Mile Point Publishing
May 2010

ISBN: 978-0-615-35692-1
Library of Congress Control Number: 2010923352
Printed in the United States of America

ACKNOWLEDGMENTS

The author would like to express his deepest appreciation and thanks to the following for their invaluable assistance in the creation of this book.

On Planet Earth: Betty Lou Kishler for proofreading, advice and simply being there. You are loved.

Spirit World: Paul, Chang, Barbara, Isabel, Patrick and Iro, a beautiful team known to me as the Love and Light Brigade. "The Quest" and this book "Insights" would not have happened without you.

And to Tom Passey, dowser extraordinaire, who shared with me his incredible insights into Cosmic Energy.

To Ken Kishler for his cover photograph.

And to all the pilgrims, students and sages who stopped by on their Paths to share wisdom.

CONTENTS

INTRODUCTION
A GIFT OF THE SPIRIT

S INCE WRITING "The Quest of the Radical Spiritualist" I have been asked by a lot of people, what is the difference between a Spiritualist and a Radical Spiritualist?

The Spiritualist believes there is no such thing as death. To be honest, there is a death. It is a death of the human body. It ceases to function. But the spirit, the soul lives on and moves on. Normally, it clears the physical world and makes a transition into the Spirit World where it continues to develop spiritually in a World that is far more complex, far more beautiful than the Earth Plain. I say "normally" because, as we shall see, some get "stuck in transition," and a rescue becomes a healing.

Spiritualists on Earth believe and practice communication with Spirits of loved ones and friends that have gone on. Even Pope Benedict said that he communicates with the former Pope now in Spirit. Spiritualists also practice spirit-directed hands-on healings in their churches and spiritual centers.

In addition they maintain a set of principles much like those proclaimed by the mainline churches, except they believe Jesus is not the Son of God, a product of an illogical virgin birth or any of the other man-made claims designed and attributed to Jesus by the Universal Church. Jesus was a great teacher, a healer and a medium. He too communicated with spirits. He too was a radical.

The problem is not the beliefs but the fact a substantial number of American and British Spiritualists plus many Spiritualist Churches are inactive socially. Some have Lyceums for the development of young people, but many others, have slipped into the dust of history. Spiritualists claim Spiritualism is a science and a philosophy, but they do little or nothing to substantiate these aspects.

Science and Philosophy need recorded data. Proving that you can communicate with loved ones every Sunday, or perform some hands-on healing where few, if any records are kept, leaves a lot to be desired. The fascination and attraction of Sunday messages becomes like the rerun of an old Cecil B. DeMille movie: it was great in its day, but now does not impress many people, particularly newcomers to the ranks..

The Radical Spiritualist has the same basic beliefs as the Spiritualist, but he and she is an activist, an explorer, a person who seeks facts and strives for scientific information. He or she learns from the masters, both worldly and in Spirit, and goes on to develop themselves. They are alert for opportunities. They use the mediumistic ability of communication to ask questions of teachers and sources in the Spirit World. They gather around them dedicated radical spiritualists whose vision is to learn, then spread the word to a hungry world.

A hungry world? Absolutely! Researchers say people are leaving the mainline churches in search of God. They ardently seek a higher, more mature view of spirituality than that offered by the spiritually bankrupt dictums written by Constantine's gang of bishops for mass-control seventeen centuries ago.

But spiritual maturity is difficult to conceive in an every-day environment where people are becoming sick through a bombardment of fears prompted by news of wars, terrorism, detection screens, swine flu, collapse of the financial system, a loss of hard earned savings, threats of socialism, corrupt politicians and mainline church abuse of children..

Many a person's confidence in the American health system is steadily being undermined by television commercials for pharmaceutical products that are supposed to heal but are accompanied by a flock of alarming contraindications. These are side effects that may maim and even kill you. They prompt even more stress, anxiety and psychological problems. Combine all this with family relations under pressure, and it is little wonder that people are stressed, anxious and popping pills like candies – pills that may have adverse effects..

It's time for Spiritualists and spiritually-minded folk to get involved in healing. But while gallant and traditional, it is not enough for Spiritualists to offer hands-on healing at church services on Sundays. Most such healing services go unannounced anyway because the emphasis is always on mediumship and messages from loved ones and friends who have crossed over.

After a few attendances, newcomers realize the Spiritualist Church is just another church, somber, sober and boringly routine. Did God, Infinite Intelligence, the Creator, the Universal Mind who created a really neat and beautiful Universe want human beings to look so damned miserable when attending church?

Laughter has long been known as a great healing modality. Spiritualist Churches and groups could start their services and meetings by including ten minute laughter sessions. This is a sure-fire way to sky-rocket energy. Why did kings, queens and knights of old have jesters? To make the flock laugh and take them out of the bleak side of life.

People are in desperate need of good, holistic healing and with it, the confidence that builds spiritual maturity. The good news is Spiritualists can offer both. There are many healing opportunities to be explored by the Radical Spiritualist bent on healing.

This book is designed to get you started on the Royal Highway or as the Spanish say El Camino Real. All healing takes place in an altered state of consciousness, in other words, one must be relaxed and focused. Don't let the idea of trance put you off. Day-dreaming is an altered state of consciousness, and so it is when you are engrossed in a movie, a theater play or opera, or reading a good book. An effective healer must be focused and in an altered state.

A would-be healer with a negative ego or False Self problem needs to dump it, or as philosopher Paul Brunton says in one of his famous Notebooks, the ego must be crucified. We talk about dissolving the ego in this book, but if the ego is a major problem, one needs to study my earlier book *Cracking the Glass Darkly* and really break free.

Our adventures through the Healing Paths pass through a number of oases for the Radical Spiritualist, such as conscious relaxation or meditation, the value of self-talk, the power of imagery, dowsing and working with pendulums, the value of finding healing through past lives (even if you do not believe in reincarnation), working with sacred sounds and sound healing, color healing, therapeutic touch, the value of spirit guides, giving comfort to the dying and a much neglected aspect spirit rescue.

For some pilgrims along the Healing Paths it may be advantageous to become "certified" but for the most part, the healing modalities offered in the book are designed for spiritually minded pilgrims who wish to extend their knowledge and "gifts of the spirit" to help heal themselves and those around them whether they are in church or privately in a home or office setting.

So what is a radical spiritualist? It is the fully conscious person who just does not only believe in spirit communications and the Afterlife, but lives with the knowledge and benefits of a higher life. The radical spiritualist may belong to a church or an organized spiritual group, or she and he may walk alone on the Healing Paths spreading love, light and knowledge. The radical spiritualist seizes every opportunity to broaden his or her understanding of God, the Universal Mind, and through developing spiritualist philosophy with scientific research and studies, work to help and heal the Human Family.

We are spiritual beings with enormous, mind-boggling potentials. As you walk and learn on the Healing Paths, the power of the human spirit will come as a powerful revelation. You may well hear or continue to hear God and spirit voices, but you will readily realize and appreciate the cosmic truth in healing. You have the power. And, always remember, Jesus the Sage of Gallilee started his ministry with a healing.

Love, Light and Blessings.

Robert Egby
Chaumont Bay, Lake Ontario
Chaumont, New York.
April 2010

1

A HEALING
SOMEWHERE IN TIME

"If we attempted all things of which we are capable,
we would literally astound ourselves."
– Thomas Edison, via Toastmasters Meeting agenda.

WE WERE RECLINING in the shade sipping the Spirit World's version of mint juleps, which an Earthly bartender would have made with bourbon and sugar over crushed ice and flavoring or garnishing with mint. Paul vowed they were non-alcoholic. The group noted my quizzical expression.

"Nothing is what it seems," Barbara noted dryly. "Particularly in the Spirit World."

"And that goes for the Universe itself," put in Isabel with a grin. Even on Earth she had possessed a devious sense of humor. "It's little wonder that the seven or so billion humans wander about in a mixed up daze."

"Let's not get into abstractions," said Paul firmly. "Robert asked us into his Sanctuary to assist with his book on healing.

"Isn't that the realm of Chang, his spiritual healing guide?" asked Barbara.

A brilliant green energy ball materialized in the seat across the wicker table. Chang, still clinging to nineteenth century fashions wears a simple purple-gray Changpao, a long gown and a neat jacket. "You called?" his old wizened face grinned.

"For readers – and Robert – where would the healing road start? Paul eyed everyone across the top of the glass.

"In the Spiritualist Church," suggested Barbara. "We had some excellent hands-on healers in our church."

"What about Harry Edwards," suggested Isabel. "Harry created the famous Spiritual Healing Sanctuary at Shere in Surrey and it attracted thousands from all over the world. Everyone wanted to be healed. He did some great work."

"Harry's been over here for some time," added Paul. He conducts energy sessions for new arrivals who still cling to their Earthly ailments."

"The ancient Greeks and the Egyptians had what they called their sleep temples," he continued. "In the fifth and fourth centuries BCE, there were over 400 such Greek institutions. The afflicted person was placed in a deep trance, similar to sleep, and the god Æsculapius would perform seemingly miraculous cures.

"Priests inducted the patients into a deep trance through chanting and toning, much the same as you perform Sound Healing. The patients would be kept in a trance state for three days, in which time they were given healing suggestions, much like you do in hypnosis these days. The temples attracted many spirits and were great places for both mental and physical healing." Paul sniffed, then added: "Of course, the whole lot was wiped out by Flavius Theodosius in AD 391, aided and abetted by the early Christian fanatics."

Chang studied a white clay pipe he enjoyed smoking. "The Chinese people have always been closer to the earth than people now. They knew the harm Geopathic Zones or Black Streams could cause to unwitting victims some 4,000 years ago and families avoided building their homes on such places. They also called them Dragon Lines." The old Chinese doctor who last lived on Earth in 1893, dug into his satchel and pulled out a piece of white bone. He showed it to the group. I asked him what it was and he gave it to me to hold.

The wizened face grinned easily. "It is an oracle bone. Made from the shoulder bones of an ox. Turtle bones also served. As you see it is covered with Chinese writing, and note there is a crack in it. A person who required the answer to a question, or needed healing with herbs, would ask a priest or a shaman. The priest would heat the bone, and how it burned and split, would then divine the answer from the bone's condition. In recent years, many such artifacts have been found in certain parts of China."

His hand reached out for the old bone. "But Robert, tell the people about the Dragon Lines – geopathic stress – because they are injuring and even killing people in many countries."

Barbara looked first at Isabel, then back to Paul: "You mentioned recently that in your research you had discovered that toning, spirit communications and imagery date back to the time of the Cro-Magnons, the people who lived in Europe as the Ice Age receded."

Paul nodded reluctantly and sighed. "Barbara, you sure like to stir things up." He stopped, paused and stared at me through grey eyes that twinkled, almost mischievously. "Robert, want to go into another dimension?"

"Like astral projection?"

"Nah! That's Psychic 101 stuff. This is a technique some of the boffins developed. You'll like it."

There was really no time to protest and counter with: "Can we do it another time?" It just happened. In a blink. Here was I meditating with my consciousness in my Sanctuary of the Mind, generally a peaceful garden, and surrounded by my spirit guides, when suddenly I was somewhere else and it was black. Dead black. A strong hand held my neck.

"Stand up. You'll feel solid ground under your feet." It was Paul. "Start walking, I will guide you."

"Where the heck are we?"

"In a cave, somewhere in Europe," he said. "If you believe in time – we are now 15,000 years back, looking for the Cro-Magnons.

"Can you see where we are going?"

"Sure. Can't you?"

"No."

"You'd better do some more work on your psychic vision." His hand zipped across my brow chakra.

Suddenly the cave broadened out and oil lamps and torches created an almost eerie, misty glow across the expanse of the cavern. A dozen human figures attired in animal furs and pelts fashioned into clothes, moved slowly across the scene, oblivious of our presence. Simple scaffolding reached up to the ceiling, and three figures were perched on top.

"What are they doing?" I asked.

"Painting, drawing," said Paul easily. "They are painting bisons. If you look through the smoke and haze you'll see more." The air seemed to clear and I spotted pictures of horses, an hyena, several lions and two more bison."

"Why are the men painting animals?"

"What makes you think they are men?" Barbara joined in from behind Paul. "The artists are women.

"Encylopedias and such always refer to cave painters as men," I put in defensively.

"Sure!" snapped Barbara, "Remnants of a male oriented society. But note this, most of the relics found in the caves belong to women but a male-oriented archeology attributed them to males."

Paul chipped in quickly. "In your practice, you teach and encourage imagery to achieve an objective. Such as, if you want a car you image yourself driving the car you desire. Well, here, the Cro-Magnon, as you call them, the women are imaging successes for the men, the hunters who are out there chasing the creatures that provide furs and pelts, meat for the families and animal fats and oils for cooking and lamps. Animal bones are used for carvings and ornaments."

As he was speaking the artists descended and everyone stood in a circle. On a fur mat spread on the dusty floor a heavily set man, gasping for breath, lay huddled, writhing in agony among warm animal blankets. The women in the circle started with a very low chant which then sounded like a long pronounced "who" It sounded more like a sigh, a soft breath that produced a long, humming hooooo.

"It's a mantra," said Chang. "Hu is a mantra of deep power. It was one of the first words of power that were sounded in the evolution of humankind. It is still used in many mystery schools, and indeed by mystics and others."

"The injured hunter was gored by a mammoth. He's lost much blood and is waiting to die," added Paul.

"Presumably this is sound healing," I suggested, but the moment I said it, I realized I was out of my depth.

"Not exactly," he said diplomatically. "They are calling for a messenger to help them. They have discovered that if they stand in certain places in the caves, and make specific sounds, a spirit-messenger will emerge and help them.

"We are watching one of the early séances," said Isabel with her usual excitement.

Somewhere in the far reaches of the cave, a small ball of light, a glittering silvery orb, started to float out of the darkness. It hovered for several seconds near the newly painted bison on the ceiling, as if reviewing it, then suddenly dropped into the center of the circle.

In the space of one second, it became transformed into a tall woman, elegant in glittering robes. She smiled as she watched the faces of the women in the circle.

"Who is she and what is she saying. I cannot hear," I said to Paul.

"Eelilith," he said. "Her name is Eeilith, and in this age she is what you would call a spirit guide or a shaman for the community. She is a messenger, an ascended teacher and healer, some might call her a goddess. In our time she is what you would call ascended. She lives and works with the god-force. Her strong points are communication and healing."

"I sense she is talking, but I cannot hear."

"You would call it telepathy. It's mind talk, much like you use in mediumship, and we use it in Spirit. The Cro-Magnons found it easier to converse in telepathy before they learned to express words and sentences orally. Spoken words are cumbersome and often misleading. In telepathy you talk in imagery, whether it represents images, suggestions or words. There are many levels and channels in telepathy. Most Earth people lack an understanding of telepathy. It's the standard communication medium in our world.

As he spoke, Eelilith's form reduced and became a beautiful orb. It quickly circled the group of women, flew low over the heads, did a tight spiral over the injured man and suddenly disappeared through his mouth into his head.

"Our hunter is being healed," said Paul softly. "It happens a lot on Earth without sick people realizing it. A spirit enters the body of a sick person, heals them, and next morning the person has made a sudden recovery."

There was a book, I told the group, called "The Scole Experiment" by Grant Solomon that told of the activities of mediums in the mid-1990s at the village of Scole in Norfolk, England. A spirit was seen to enter the body of one of the researchers and conduct a healing.

"Same sort of thing," said Paul with a smile. "There's nothing under new the sun."

Eelilith suddenly reappeared as an orb out of the hunter's stomach. She flew round the circle again, hovered for a few seconds in front of Paul, then enveloped my head with an incredible light. A soft but commanding voice announced: "You will remember everything of this healing, and you will mention the women. They need recognition, Robert."

In a second the goddess was gone. My head felt as if a thousand photographers' flash bulbs had gone off. Paul steadied me. "You may like to know the hunter is standing up now and is completely healed."

"That's a miracle" said Isabel. "She performed a miracle."

Paul smiled. "Not true. You just have to work on your understanding of energy." He paused, then added: "Eelilith is a messenger. She carried and applied God's healing. It is good to remember, dear ones, that all healing comes from God."

Another flash and I was back in my Sanctuary of the Mind, Paul and the others had gone. I brought myself to full waking consciousness in my home. Thirsty, I walked to the kitchen for a drink, and as I passed the bathroom mirror, I stopped and looked at my face. It was incredibly tanned as if I had been in the hot sun all day.

2

RELAXATION,
THE KEY TO GOOD HEALTH

Cicero, the great Roman orator once said:
"A happy life begins with the tranquility of the mind."

"**T**RANCE! You won't get me into no damned trance. Nobody is going to control my mind," snorted the smoker one day. "I'm in charge of my head and that's that."

"Sir, if you are in charge of your mind, you can quit smoking all by yourself, quite easily," said the therapist firmly. "Good-bye!"

Just about everyone on the planet goes into trance states several times a minute. It is called daydreaming and it happens when a person has a break and finds there is nothing to do. Perhaps they are waiting for a bus, or sitting on a train and staring through a window, or maybe sitting in an office waiting for a call. Daydreaming occurs without our being conscious of it, and normally concludes when we realize the condition, and snap out of the state. It is a natural human state.

Daydreaming is an elementary form of meditation or self-hypnosis. It happens when the energy frequency of the brain quietly slips down from a Beta state to an Alpha state, It's normally a visionary experience featuring pleasant thoughts of something past or something in the future. Daydreaming is never in the Here and Now. It usually takes the day-dreamer away from his or her immediate environment into something positive.

People watching a person daydreaming often make fun of them or make deriding comments such as "He's off on a different planet again" But daydreaming is also very useful for creative people such as designers and architects, composers and authors, movie-makers, research scientists and others. Daydreaming can be a vey positive meditative state. Nevertheless, it is recognized as a trance state, and it does open the gate to a whole new world of healthy living and healing. Why? Because it relaxes.

UNDERSTANDING BRAIN WAVES AND ENERGY

Some years ago, I explained brain waves and energy to an eighty-three year old lady named Tillie who could not understand why she kept on nodding off and "having some nice dreams with my sweetheart" and then coming back to full consciousness. "Charlie's been dead twenty years, so what is going on in my upper storey?" So here's what I explained.

In a nutshell there are four classification levels of brain waves and they are called Beta, Alpha, Theta and Delta. Let's look at each one, because it helps to understand meditation and healing and life in general.

Beta waves: These are fast paced and flow at the rate of between 14 and 30 cycles per second (CPS). Most people in their daily lives have an average beta level of 20. This level rises and falls depending on activities, emotions such as excitement, anxiety and stress. Impatience, enthusiasm, anger, ecstasy, fear and jealousy can and do play havoc with Beta waves.

People in careers and activities governed by time and space normally have elevated brain wave activity. If this activity is sustained for excessive periods over months and years, the person suffers burnout or catastrophic sickness.

Prolonged high brain wave activity reduces the body's immune system and resistance to disease.

Metaphysical activity such as meditation, self-hypnosis, spirit communication rarely if ever take place in the Beta state. Self-healing or natural healing is slow to take effect in Beta which is why health professionals will tell a sick patient to "go home and rest." Doing nothing takes one out of Beta and slips you into Alpha.

Alpha waves: This is the category where brain waves vibrate between 8 and 13 cycles. Daydreams, meditation, self-hypnosis and conscious relaxation all take place at various levels in Alpha. Mediums and healers work in this state because Alpha is great for conscious healing – and prayer and contacting spirits.

This is the region of the creators – writers, artists, composers, photographers and others. Alpha allows concentration and selective focusing. Many progressive students study in this state. Memory retention and memory access are enhanced here.

Have you ever wondered why young children learn so quickly? The fact is most children live in the Alpha state until they are seven or eight years old. This is the reason why some parents fail to communicate well with young children because the elder is in active Beta and the child is the relaxed Alpha. Want to communicate with your child? Relax in Alpha and start communicating on the child's level. Children in Alpha find it easy to see spirits and psychic phenomena.

If you are into metaphysics and wish to communicate with loved ones or friends and spirit guides on the Other Side, you had better be in trance in the Alpha state, because in Beta will not work.

Have you ever wondered after driving home, how you got there so quickly, or while reading a book or watching an engrossing movie, time just disappeared, but you felt good afterwards. Chances are you were in alpha.

The alpha state is ideal for reducing stress and anxiety and accelerating healing. More on this later.

Theta waves: These waves vibrate at between 4 to 7 CPS and this state is ideal for deep meditation and self-hypnosis. Also most of our dreams occur in Theta. Everyone passes through this state of consciousness on the way to sleep and returns through Theta when waking up in the morning. Dreams, good and bad take place in Theta. Conscious Theta meditation is an excellent basis for reducing blood pressure (hypertension), pulse rate and visualizing improved circulation. It is also ideal for creative people searching for ideas in the Cosmos, astral travel and out of body experiences, and for psychic researchers. (I was in theta when we traveled back in time to the Cro-Magnons in the previous chapter.)

One of the downsides of meditating in Theta is the inclination to "trip out" or go to sleep and miss your objective especially performing imagery. If this is the case, practice meditation sitting upright in a chair and work to stay in Alpha.

Delta waves: Brain wave activity drops to between 2 and 7 CPS and is the region of deep sleep. This is where total rest, rejuvenation and recuperation occur. Dreams are rare, and researchers say we normally sleep in Theta, but we drop down into Delta several times during the course of a good night's sleep. Prolonged stay in Delta rarely occurs, except for people recovering from serious mental or physical injury. Again, lack of Delta sleep can result in serious disorders. Also astral travel does occur in this state, which is why many people fail to consciously recall what their souls did during the night.

As we tread the Healing Road let us discuss relaxation.

WHAT IS RELAXATION?

Contrary to what most people think, relaxation does not mean feeling sleepy. It does not mean stationary as opposed to moving. It is not about doing nothing, or being lazy, or putting less effort into something. You can be wide awake and perfectly relaxed. You can be moving quickly and expending energy and still be relaxed. You could even be engaged in intense physical combat and be supremely relaxed. All in Alpha.

Relaxation is the basis of meditation, self-hypnosis and conscious relaxation. You might wish to know that all hypnosis, the clinical stuff administered by a doctor or a certified hypnotherapist, is always self-hypnosis. You cannot be hypnotized against your will. You must wish or consciously allow it to happen.

Now, having said that, you should also realize that when you watch a movie, read a good book, take in a good show at the theater, you are normally in a light Alpha trance state.

This is why the Madison Avenue advertising gurus plant their messages on popular television shows. The trade is fully conscious that millions of people are totally unaware they are viewing television in a highly receptive altered state of consciousness and that is a powerful mode for teaching.

While on the subject, you might like to know that the subconscious mind never sleeps. You might be fast asleep on the sofa while the television is still working and your subconscious mind is faithfully listening to all those commercials. The subconscious learns through repetition. So now you know why commercials are frustratingly repeated. It's all to influence your mind.

STRESS, THE SILENT KILLER

If you spend much of your day in the Beta state, chances are you are suffering some level of stress. Life in many of the so-called advanced countries has substantially increased its pace in the last fifty years, and with technology spearheading the way, life is not expected to get slower any time soon. In other words, the need to handle stress is becoming more and more acute as the days pass.

Many jobs require workers to hide their true feelings, so they never get a chance to sound off, not unless they wish to find another mode of employment. People with high stress can be found in such work as teaching, medicine, social services, fire fighting and rescue, law enforcement and customer service. Others are found in information technology, any of the fields of finance, engineering, sales and marketing, and in legal secretarial work.

Various studies clearly show that high stress jobs frequently result in overeating, smoking, excessive drinking of coffee (caffeine) and / or alcohol, increased blood pressure, yielding to sickness and depression, or break-up of relationships or worse – suicide.

On April 28th 2008, Newsweek reported that every year, between 300 and 400 doctors take their own lives. That's roughly one a day. No other profession has a higher suicide rate.

Our lifestyle, it seems, is creating more havoc in our lives than any terrorist planning an attack on this country.

But stress in the Beta state is not restricted to working adults, sometimes teens feel so depressed they consider ending their lives, reports Mental Health America. Each year, almost 5,000 young people, ages 15 to 24, kill themselves. The rate of suicide for this age group has nearly tripled since 1960, making it the third leading cause of death in adolescents and the second leading cause of death among college age youth. Independent experts say apparent insecurity, rapid life changes, confusing cultures and ideologies, and persistent alarm and despondency in the news media create chronic stress in young minds.

In all of this, the multi-billion dollar pharmaceutical industry plies its lucrative wares after being promoted by commercials that always say "check with your doctor" which is a great way of saying, if the doctor gives it to you, it must be good. Yes, there is a place for pharmaceutical products in our lives, but it has become a growing obsession, an elixir, a remedy for stress and all that ails you.

Growing numbers of doctors are prescribing relaxation, meditation and imagery training when patients are suffering from chronic stress and sickness. However these should be taught at an early age, ready for the pressures of life that lie ahead. Looking at the stress that plagues society today, one wonders how inept our leaders were, not to have openly and actively promoted it for the younger people. They could have saved billions of dollars in health care and a lot of lives.

THE PHYSICAL BENEFITS OF RELAXATION

There are many health benefits to be gained from spending fifteen or twenty minutes each day, or even five days a week, in some form of relaxation.

First of all, relaxation in any altered state of consciousness will effectively slow down your heart rate. Now, if there's any muscle in your entire body that needs some TLC – tender loving care – it's your heart muscle. The average pulse rate in an adult male is about 72 BPM, while the average for an adult woman is 76 to 80. Stress and anxiety fuel the heart rate to go higher. When you relax on a regular basis, you will find that in many cases the pulse rate can drop to 60 to 65. Think about it. When you relax you are giving your heart muscle longer to rest in-between pumping blood. That's a neat investment. In dollars it costs nothing, and it takes just a few minutes of your time. What a deal!

Relaxation or trance meditation can, in many cases, lower your blood pressure, and cause your breathing rate to slow down because your body needs less oxygen. The Mayo Clinic points out that relaxation can also increase blood flow to major muscles, reduce muscle tension and chronic pain, improve concentration, reduce anger and frustration, and boost your confidence to handle problems.

SEND YOUR BODY A MESSAGE

There is a pronounced feeling among many people that relaxation is just being lazy, getting out of things. They feel they will not have enough energy to work, and will, perhaps, be laid off. Well, just the reverse is true. When you perform conscious relaxation, meditation, self-hypnosis or Yoga, the body, mind and spirit have time to recuperate.

These activities in altered states of consciousness are not sleeping. It is a time when you are sending a message to your body such as: *" I am totally relaxed. I am recuperating and being restored to optimal health. I say this in an aura of love and blessings."* Say it several times with conviction *and y*ou will find that when you arise, you have more energy than

17

before. In addition, you will feel more alert, and are able to focus and exercise creative in any activity.

RELAXATION MADE EASY

A very simple way of relaxing is concentrating on your breathing and you can do this anywhere when you need a few moments to let go. It comes from Buddhism. When you concentrate on your breathing for a while, your body becomes relaxed and your mind becomes peaceful.

- Sit in a comfortable position with your back straight.
- Place your hands in your lap with the left hand on the bottom.
- Keep your eyelids half-closed.
- Concentrate on the tip of your nose. Notice your breathing coming and going.
- After a few minutes, take one slow deep breath and as you breathe out say out loud: "*Wide awake!*" and be wide awake.

Now, you can go on and experience a more comprehensive technique for letting go.

MUSCLES: SIMPLE BUT EFFECTIVE

This technique is an oldie but goodie. Fine a place where you will not be disturbed. Sit in a chair with your back fairly erect, head looking forward. Hands unclasped on your lap, fingers loose. Close your eyes and mentally focus on your body. Do not try to change anything.

In this technique you mentally observe your body doing its job, breathing in oxygen and breathing out carbon dioxide. Resist any judging or casting an opinion on how well or how bad you are doing.

Do this for two or three minutes, and you will notice as you finish, your breathing, your heart rate will have slowed down, and you will feel completely relaxed, restored and ready to get on with the business of living.

But think about this. What have you done? Basically nothing, you simply observed your body. And incredibly, it started to slow down.

MUSCLE TENSING EXERCISE

The technique of progressive muscle tensing for relaxation dates back to the 1930s and a physician named Edmund Jacobsen who founded Progressive Muscle Relaxation and Biofeedback. Progressive muscle relaxation can be learned by just about anyone and requires only ten to 20 minutes a day to practice. (If you have muscle problems check the last paragraph in this section)

This technique will have you tensing and relaxing the muscle groups one at a time in a specific order, generally beginning with the lower extremities and ending with the face, abdomen, and chest. It's best if you find yourself a place to lie down, either on a bed or sofa, or even a recliner.

Always wear loose comfortable clothing in any relaxation exercise, and never, ever hurry.

Now, while slowly breathing in, contract one muscle group. You might select your thighs or lower leg muscles, or even your feet. Tense the muscles for five to ten seconds, then exhale and suddenly release the tension in that muscle group. Give yourself perhaps twenty seconds to relax, and then move on to the next set of muscles.

OBSERVE ANY CHANGES

As you release the tension, observe the changes you feel in the muscles and in your body generally as the muscle group is relaxed. If you want, mentally image any tension flowing down and away from your body as you relax in-between muscle tensing. Gradually and systematically work your way up your body contracting and relaxing different muscle groups.

Incidentally, this exercise is great for many insomniacs. Simply rest in bed and perform progressive muscle relaxation. Soon, you will find that you slip off into a deep healthy sleep.

As you practice this exercise on a daily basis, you will find symptoms of stress and anxiety fading out of your life, and your world will start to feel better. Also, when doing this exercise, observe if the body is telling you anything you need to know, but have not consciously suspected.

Another point, if you suffer from any muscle afflictions or rheumatic illness, check with your doctor first. As a hypnotherapist, I normally suggest people with rheumatoid arthritis refrain from this exercise and go more with the image relaxation techniques which are coming up.

EXERCISE: BREATHING AND IMAGERY

Find yourself a quiet place where you will not be disturbed. Close any telephones and inform any people in the house that you are relaxing. It helps if the room has reduced light, like drapes drawn in daylight, or a soft light at night. Perhaps you might like a candle. Incense can be a good aid to relaxation too. Sandalwood is easy going. Perform this exercise either sitting up in a chair, or resting in a recliner or on a bed. You might enjoy lying on the floor on a carpet with your head on a pillow. It's your choice, simply be comfortable.

Close your eyes, and just imagine you have nothing to do, nowhere to go, nothing to think about just to relax. Now, gently focus on your breathing. When you are ready, image or think that the next breath you breathe in is full of relaxation and it is invading your body through your lungs.

Now as you breathe out, imagine, just imagine all that relaxation is going down to your feet. Imagine your feet are relaxing.

Wait a couple of breaths, and then with the next breath, send the relaxation all the way down to your shins and calf muscles, and imagine those muscles are relaxing. Do this for all parts of your body, the thighs, the abdomen, your hips, waist, back, chest, hands, arms, shoulders, neck, head and face.

For the last breath, imagine that you are flooding all of your body with relaxation. One word of advice: Never, ever hurry relaxation, meditation, self-hypnosis, yoga or whatever. Always remember, whatever you imagine actually happens.

Perform this simple exercise and you will undoubtedly feel the healing process starting, and if you persist, the healing will intensify. Your stress and anxiety levels will drop, you will feel more in charge of yourself, the world will start to look a better place, you will sleep better, and have the opportunity of rebuilding relationships.

GOING DEEPER AND DEEPER

No two states of relaxation are alike, and there will be a time when you wish to go deeper. Here's a technique taught by one of my first hypnosis teachers, the knowledgeable Dr. A.M. Krasner who toured the country doing training seminars. His book *The Wizard Within* is an excellent training manual.

To go deeper into trance, just imagine or visualize a large blackboard in front of you. You have a piece of chalk in your hand and you begin to write the alphabet, one letter at a time, beginning with the large letter A. When you have written your A, erase it and then write a large letter B. See yourself as you erase the B, then proceed to write the next letter C. Keep on writing and erasing, writing and erasing and mentally saying to yourself: *"Every time I erase a letter I go deeper and deeper into relaxation."* If your conscious mind "trips out" and forgets what you are doing, just pick up the alphabet wherever you think you left off. Keep on writing and erasing and going deeper. When you have reached a depth that feels right, stay at that depth for the rest of your session.

COMING BACK TO FULL CONSCIOUSNESS

When you have been in an altered state for twenty minutes or so and wish to return to normal consciousness, perform the following technique.

Take in a slow deep breath, and as you breathe out slowly, say slowly and deliberately, *"Wide awake! I am now wide-awake."* Or you can do the following by saying to yourself: *"At the count of five I will be wide awake – one – two – three – four – five. Wide awake!"*

All this of course raises the question: *"What to do in those periods of relaxation or meditation?"* The answer comes next.

3

CREATING A
SANCTUARY OF THE MIND

ONE OF THE MOST POWERFUL and effective strategies to assist and encourage personal healing is to create a Sanctuary of the Mind. Performed in an altered state of consciousness, whether it is meditation, self-hypnosis or simple conscious relaxation, a Sanctuary of the Mind will enhance creative healing in many aspects. Your mind is close to the peak of creativity and healing when you are in any relaxed state. When you get the hang of it, relaxing or imagining in the Sanctuary of the Mind becomes quite easy, very effective and wonderfully appealing.

Before creating the Sanctuary make sure you are comfortable. Simply think of yourself letting go of any stress, any tensions that have no place in your life.

A Sanctuary of the Mind belongs to you. It is totally private, and no one – I repeat, no one – is allowed in your Sanctuary, unless they are invited by you, and then, they must enter by their own "vistor" gateway. When their visit is complete, they will either leave of their own accord, or at your request. You are always in charge in your Sanctuary.

The Sanctuary location is totally up to you. You can make it as big or as small as you wish. If it starts being small, do not be concerned, you always have the option to expand it.

Your Sanctuary can be anywhere your heart desires. Allow it to be your creation. You will be surprised at how creative your mind can be once you get started.

Some students have created sanctuaries on private tropical islands in the Pacific, a plateau high in the alps, a clearing deep in the forest, an island in the middle of a beautiful lake, and even a private old-world castle overlooking a majestic landscape of waterfalls and rivers coursing down valleys and gorges to the sea. Or it might be a secluded sandy beach overlooking a perfectly blue sea. Sanctuaries are always places of peace and beauty.

When you first create a Sanctuary of the Mind, do not be concerned that it appears so simple. Some of the most elementary sanctuaries have brought their owners extremely positive results.

As you visit your Sanctuary on a regular basis, you will find changes happening without warning. Things, such as trees, streams and bridges may move, or the flowers that were not doing well yesterday, are splendiferous today displaying a multitude of colors. Remember, a Sanctuary of the Mind is a living part of you and changes in occur quite often. It is simple evolution. Remember, you have evolved from the person you were yesterday and tomorrow you will be different from the person you are today. Simply observe any changes in the Sanctuary without judging.

SETTING UP A SPECIAL PLACE

One more point. It's advisable to have a Special Place in your Sanctuary. A Special Place is a base camp, a grounding point, a home, a launch pad for performing an exercise, or going on a mental excursion or having a spiritual rendezvous. The Place can be a bench, a recliner, a hammock stretched between two trees, a mat on the earth, or even a soft grassy or sandy bank. It is the place where you start and finish your meditation or hypnosis session. This is the place where you say to yourself: "I have nothing to do, nowhere to go, nothing to think about, just relax."

Always remember, just by being in your Sanctuary is a stress-reducer. If you do nothing else but relax there for 15 minutes and observe the scenery, it will start to produce benefits.

ENTRIES AND EXITS

It is always a good idea to have two entry points in your Sanctuary. One is for you and the other is for your visitors, such as Spirit Guides, Spirit Healers, Angels, Messngers and Loved ones from the Higher Levels. We will deal with this aspect later.

Your own entry point can be a simple garden gate which you open and close, or it might be something exotic like a door deploying fingerprint or iris reading security systems. Personally, I prefer the simple garden gate although at one time I used to have an old wooden fence with a style for climbing over. I prefer a simple, rustic Sanctuary with matching entrance points.

AN ARCHWAY WITH A LOVE VIBRATION

If you are a beginner and not quite sure of yourself, the second entry point is a necessary requirement. For starters I suggest an archway. It can be an ancient arch made of stones or marble, or a modern archway built of concrete, granite or if you feel rich, have an arch made of polished titanium. It's your choice. A necessary adjunct is to have a beam of pure white cosmic energy completely surrounding the arch, and the beam of light is always on a love vibration. Everyone who enters your Sanctuary has to pass through this beam of cosmic energy.

Occasionally, an uninvited personality may well appear. For instance, a young woman complained to me that every time she arrived in her Sanctuary, her mother – still very much alive and walking the Earth – would appear. In therapy, she cut her psychic ties with her very possessive and dominant mother. These things happen. As my old friend and colleague Tom Passey used advise students to say: *"If any negative energy comes towards me it is immediately transmuted and converted into positive, loving energy."* The point of this is to reinforce your self-confidence when spirits are invited to come to visit.

CUTTING A PSYCHIC TIE

How do you cut a psychic tie? See yourself in your Sanctuary with the person with whom you wish to sever your psychic tie. Have them standing about thirty yards away. See a string or cord stretching between your brow chakra, that's the third eye in your forehead, just above the bridge of the nose, and their third eye. You are also armed with a pair of scissors in your hand.

This is where you need to be assertive and in charge. You have made up your mind to sever your psychic tie. There is no explanation, no reasons. Just do it.

State the following, or something similar: *"There is no need for us to be psychically connected and I am Now cutting the tie that binds us. You go your way and I am going my way. Go with love and light."* At this point raise the scissors and cut the string or cord. The other person will promptly disappear from your Sanctuary.

THE POWER TO MAKE IT REAL

The essential thing about a Sanctuary of the Mind is to make it real. If you have trouble mentally imaging a garden, go to one of the great horticultural gardens and sit there for a while, absorbing all you see and feel. A good, well developed and maintained park offers a similar opportunity. The same applies if your Sanctuary is on a remote and secluded sandy beach, or a meadow, a castle, a mountain, visit a similar location, if you can, and quietly observe everything around you. If you're on a sandy beach, sit there and allow the sand to run through your fingers. Feel that sand in your mind.

A young woman attending one of my workshops, said: "I can't image a tree." I looked out the window. A large oak was across the lawn. "Go to that tree, put your hands on the trunk and really get the feel of the bark." Twenty minutes later, she returned. "That's fascinating. Now I can see the tree in my mind."

Talking of trees, they are great for building energy, healing and restoring weakened immune systems.

EXERCISE: THE HEALING TREE

When you are established in your Sanctuary of the Mind, create a special tree, something in your mind that resembles healing, strength and vitality. You might wish to select an oak tree. It is a common symbol of strength and endurance and has been chosen as the national tree of a number of countries throughout the world. Oaks are also the state trees of Connecticut, Illinois, Maryland, Prince Edward Island, New Jersey and Georgia. In history, the druids held their worship ceremonies under oak trees. The mighty oak does have a special power. But you can select any strong tree, just make sure it is a symbol of strength and power.

In your Sanctuary feel yourself standing close to the tree. Imagine raising your hands and placing them on the trunk. Allow your fingers to explore its bark. This is a wonderful imagery exercise. When you feel comfortable, gaze up through the branches of this great oak and observe the hundreds, perhaps thousands of leaves silhouetted against the blue sky.

Sense or believe that the Cosmos, the Universe is full of powerful, loving, cosmic healing energy and it is yours for the asking. Remember the words of the teacher: *"Ask and you shall receive."* Well, it's time to ask. Know that those thousands of leaves silhouetted against the sky are collectors or receptors of powerful cosmic healing energy and they are working for you.

Next, imagine that vital force, that wonderful loving, healing energy is flowing from the leaves through the upper branches, cascading down through the big branches down into the main trunk of the tree. As the energy reaches the level of your hands, it swirls like a powerful stream through your fingers and palms and arms into your body. Allow it to flood your entire being. Sense it, feel it. Imagine it flowing firmly and powerfully to your head, shoulders, arms, legs and torso. Parts of your body may well tingle, even become warm. Keep the energy running and know that any negative cell, any negative part of you is being transmuted and converted into a positive, healthy, vibrant part of your body. Allow the energy to flow like a stream, a river through your body before it flows into the ground.

This is one of the most powerful healing and revitalization exercises that anyone can perform. Maintain the flow for several minutes, or until your higher self concludes you have had enough for today. If you are sick, perform this exercise several times a day until you feel better.

When you have completed the exercise, return to your Special Place in your Sanctuary and relax for several minutes before coming back to full waking consciousness. One final point: Always thank the Creator, the Universe, the Cosmos or whoever you pray to for the healing.

Before we move on, you do not have to be sick to benefit from relaxing in a Sanctuary of the Mind. In fact, systematic relaxation performed on a regular basis, say twenty minutes a day for five days a week, can work wonders for wellness, reducing chronic stress, tension and normally strengthening the body's immune system.

OTHER THINGS TO DO IN YOUR SANCTUARY

If you are sick or recuperating from a sickness or an operation, you will probably need to create a Healing Center in your Sanctuary. Some people image Grecian, Roman or even pagan temples while others enjoy small amphitheaters with a marble or granite healing table in the center.

One type, popular among rustic-minded folk is having a small, intimate old-world cottage surrounded by herbs and flowers. Another is a spa where the flowing waters reduce chronic pain and instigate healing. We will be writing about the curative powers of water in healing, later on the Healing Path.

It is important to know that the key to effective healing is imagery. I have said it many times at workshops and you have experienced it by the exercises in this book: *"Whatever you imagine in your body actually happens. If you imagine you are well, you will be well, if you imagine you are sick you will be sick and if you imagine you are relaxed, you will be relaxed."* The challenge now is to imagine you are beating a disease and are getting well.

THE CANCEROUS TUMOR

Some years ago, I had a client named Tim (not his real name) suffring from lung cancer. The condition cropped up unexpectedly quite a few years after he had stopped smoking. His doctor told of a cancerous tumor in one lung and favored surgery and a date was being set.

Visiting my center, and in conscious relaxation, Tim created a Sanctuary of the Mind on a rocky coastline near a volcano which was spewing red hot lava into the ocean. Tim watched as powerful waves quelled the heat of the lava. *"I can do that!"* he declared.

In his mind, Tim placed the red hot cancerous tumor on a rocky ledge. Each day he spent two twenty-minute sessions imaging the powerful waves dowsing the fire of his cancer and making it smaller and smaller. A month later x-rays showed the tumor greatly diminished, and two weeks later the tumor was nowhere to be found.

Tim's great quality was his passion and desire to be free of cancer and a dogged determination to see it happen. There is an inclination for some people, newly diagnosed with cancer to give up and slip into depression. Remember, your body is the temple of your soul, never give up. You have the power to fight invasions in your body. Imagination! Use it!One word of caution in imagery, never make the cancer or disease bigger than it is, in fact never make any affliction you are working to eliminate, bigger than it is. A larger than life sickness can have an adverse impact on any healing.

For instance, some disease sufferers image St. Michael on his trusty steed, armed with a lance, fighting the fire-breathing dragon representing cancer. Some imagers in their enthusiasm may be inclined to have big, terrible dragons the size of Godzilla. Wrong! Resist this and have the dragon a reasonable size and logically destructible.

A HERO LOOKING FOR TIME

Another former smoker plagued with a growing cancerous lump in his throat, asked if imagery in hypnosis would help while he waited to see a doctor. I sensed Don initially did not have the desire and passion to mount a successful imagery compaign, but during the consultation interview, he mentioned he had served in Viet Nam. A casual remark revealed he had been involved with flame-throwers.

"We regularly conducted search and clear thrusts into Commie-held territory, using flame throwers to flush the Cong from their tunnels," he said. *"Worked great! I can still see those flames twenty-five years later."* Talking aroused him. Here was the missing passion. In therapy I had him, armed and moving down a tunnel – the trachea – searching for the cancer. Wooof! He blasted the invading disease with the bravado and enthusiasm of a John Wayne. The flame-thrower scorched the enemy time and time again.

Don went home and continued sessions by himself in his Sanctuary of the Mind. Preparing for surgery, the doctor told him *"There's nothing there."* After that I didn't hear from him for two years. One day, he called. *"Thanks for giving me time to see my little girl happily married,"* he said over the telephone.

I sensed something was wrong. *"The cancer has come back. They call it metastasis – it's all over my body."*

"Tom, where's your flame-thrower?" I asked.

"It just doesn't work any more. It did for what I wanted, to see my little girl married and that was important to me," he said quietly. *"I guess the passion and the desire which you told me about so many times is all gone."*

"We can refuel, resurrect it," I urged, *"we can help..."*

His voice cut in: *"Robert, I'm tired of fighting. It's time to go and join my buddies who never came home. I just wanted to say – thanks. Thanks for what you did."* The line went dead. A month later his obituary was in the newspaper. Don never told me he had been awarded a purple heart for bravery in Viet Nam. In his way, he had been a hero looking for time.

Don's weapon against a disease had been his old flame-thrower. Tim had used the sea to cleanse himself. In all of us, there is something, some idea, some thought that will reinforce healing imagery. If there is a dire need, and the passion to succeed, your creative mind will come up with the right imagery.

EXERCISE: THE GOLDEN SUN TECHNIQUE

One excellent technique for healing minor pains and sickness in the body is called the Golden Sun exercise.

Find a place in your Sanctuary where you can image yourself lying flat on your back. When you are comfortable, create in the blue sky above, a beautiful golden sun, and know that it is beaming down healing energy into your body. Feel it, sense it. Your body may start to feel warm and start tingling. Allow the healing energy of the golden sun to penetrate every muscle, every bone, every gland, every organ, every cell of your body. As the healing energy penetrates your body, all stress, all tension dissipates. Allow the healing to continue for several minutes.

If you have a particular ailment such as a torn muscle or an ache, image a beam of light from the golden sun and focus it on the affected area. Hold it there for several minutes. When you feel the time is ready, let the golden sun go and rest in your Sanctuary for several minutes before arising and getting on with your life. Do this regularly until you feel well. As always, thank the Cosmos, the Universe or whoever you pray to.

LETTING GO OF PAIN

That headline may seem very attractive if you are anxious to let go of a physical pain, so before we embark on the next technique, a few words of caution.

Pain is a messenger and should always be taken seriously because it is part of your body's alert and warning system. Therefore, always check with a health professional before reducing or moving pain.

For instance, if you are plagued by headaches and they continue even after you have done any of the healing exercises mentioned before in this book, check with your health professional, because most of the exercises mentioned before will normally ease the tension and stress of headaches.

The following exercise is for people with muscle aches, elementary or chronic arthritis, rheumatism and fibromyalgia.

EXERCISE: THE POOL OF LETTING GO

In your Sanctuary of the Mind, create a beautiful running stream with water that comes from a spring in the mountains. You know the water is crystal clear and carries powerful healing minerals. It helps tremendously to "love" water. Appreciate the powers of water.

Dr. Masaru Emoto, the Japanese scientist who has done much to test and record the spiritual consciousness of water, says water is part of the rhythm of life. In his books he clearly demonstrates that prayers or loving words spoken over water, have a profound healing effect on it. He authored *The Secret Life of Water* with some incredible photos. So remember, it helps to love and appreciate water, whether you are drinking it, or imagining it in your Sanctuary of the Mind.

Start the exercise by thinking of yourself walking down the path to the stream and finding a pool with golden sand or fine pebbles.

Your Sanctuary is totally private, so think of yourself disrobing and wading into the pool. If you find this a little uncomfortable, see yourself in a swimsuit. You find the water is just the right temperature for you. There are some large rocks just a few feet under water, and you find you can sit on one, and even lay back so that your body is completely immersed up to your neck.

Continue to relax in this crystal clear water. Feel the power of the water, caressing, comforting, gently massaging all parts of your body. As someone once told me: *"It's as if scores of gentle angels are giving me a heavenly massage."* Allow it to happen.

When you are ready, focus your attention on your discomfort. Sense or feel it being withdrawn from your body. The water is sapping your discomfort away, totally and easily. If you can give the discomfort a color, see that color coming out of your body and flowing away. Tell the discomfort: *"I release you. Leave my body....and go with love and light."*

Finally, image the part of your body where the discomfort had been, now totally free. Know that any remnants of discomfort are being transmuted into all that is good and lovable.

To close, tell yourself slowly and deliberately: *"I love and appreciate my body."* Repeat it three times. Then continue to relax enjoying the pool, and when you are ready, step out, dry yourself and get dressed and return to your Special Place.

The Pool of Letting Go is one of the best and most comforting exercises for healing and letting go of stress and tension that has come our way. Enjoy. We will talk more about the healing powers of water as we walk the Healing Paths.

4

SELF TALK? ARE YOU CRAZY?

A RATHER LEAN, beady-eyed, unshaven, disheveled fellow walked into my Squamish office one day, slumped unceremoniously into the big recliner and announced: *"I hate to tell anyone this, but I'm a loser, I don't fit in anywhere, my kids say I'm ugly, my wife, the love of my life abandoned me, my quack doctor gave me some stuff that doesn't work, so I want you to know the world is an unhappy place."*

Clients usually take about half an hour in consultation to reveal all those points. They all fell out of him in thirty seconds. His name was Jon.

"That's pretty powerful self-talk you have there."

Jon eyed me suspiciously. "What do you mean? Self-talk?"

"It's what you say to yourself, and you repeat it, and because you keep saying it, you become that way. That's self-talk."

"Self-talk? Are you crazy?" Jon grated. "That's stupid!" Sighing, he got up and headed for the door.

"If you leave you'll always be a loser, ugly, not able to fit in, not able to hold a love in your life," I said. "Your medicine will never work and the world will always be an unhappy place."

His beady eyes stared back, hesitating. "You can change all this? People hate me?"

"They don't hate you, it's just the way you see things, and we can change your view."

"With self-talk?"

"Mostly. With self-talk," I said, then added: "Émile Coué would have loved you as a patient."

Cooey? Who the heck is he?

In a moment, but first...

MANAGING YOUR BODY

You have two types of mind in your body. The conscious mind and the subconscious mind.

The conscious mind comes into being when you awake in the morning and disappears when you fall asleep at night. Its function is necessary but limited. It is your daily guide. It analyzes, judges and is the executive director of your corporation. It makes decisions.

The subconscious mind is the manager of your body. It hands the administrative crew and manages everything there is to manage in your body. It has a seemingly unlimited memory and it remembers everything that happens with you and your environment from day one in your life.

If someone in your early life told you *"You are clumsy and boring. No one will ever love you."* And that hurtful message was repeated frequently in your early life, it would become a major element in the way the subconscious mind manages your body. First, you might start to act clumsily and feel you are inadequate, boring and unloved. Even years later as an adult such a person may well sabotage and terminate a great relationship opportunity because he or she believes *"no one will ever love me."* This is a simplification, but hopefully you will get my point.

People hurt from a whole encyclopedia of reasons, and all they want to do is lash out and say something that makes someone else hurt, even a loved one. If you have lived in a negative environment at home or at work, you will start to reflect those negative statements and worse still, you will start to identify with and live those negative statements.

There's a Universal Law called the Law of Attraction which says you will attract to you whatever you see in yourself. Negative people attract negative people. Positive people attract positive people. Poor people attract poor people. Rich people attract.... well, you know how it is.

And so to Émile Coué.

THE FRENCH CONNECTION

If you think negatively about anything, it will be negative. Émile Coué made a fascinating observation that is as important today as it was over a century ago. He observed that many people who thought negatively about their medicines did not feel the benefits. He then discovered that if a patient thinks positively about their medicines, healing is accelerated.

Coué was born in France and worked as an apothecary in the latter part of the 19th century and early 20th century. He became known for reassuring his clients by making positive comments and suggestions about the medicine's efficiency. He would also leave a small note, always positive, with each medication.

The curious Coué tracked the patients to whom he had made positive remarks about their medicine. Medicine users, people he had praised, showed noticeable improvement when compared to patients to whom nothing had been said. It was from this fascinating phenomena that Coué started to explore the use of altered states of consciousness and the power of the imagination.

THE NEED FOR POSITIVE HEALING THOUGHTS

Most people, even today, dwell on their illness, and repeatedly tell others of their plight. Coué discovered that if people replaced *"thoughts of illness"* with *"thoughts of curing and healing"* and these were repeated enough times for them to take root in the subconscious, they received accelerated healing.

The method became known as "positive auto-suggestion" or as we call it today "self-talk." However, Coué observed and noted a serious drawback. He found the main obstacle to auto-suggestion was willpower. In order to get his technique to work the patient must refrain from making any negative remarks, in other words, the patient must not let the will, the negative ego or the False Self, impose its own views on positive suggestions.

The French chemist insisted that everything must be done to ensure the positive suggestion is consciously and subconsciously accepted by the patient. Otherwise one may well end up with a harmful reverse effect. This later triggered Sigmund Freud to state that if it comes to a test between the human will and the human imagination, the imagination will always win.

For example, a person completing the written test for a driving license finds he has forgotten one of the answers, he will likely self-talk "I have forgotten the answer." The more he or she tries to come up with the answer, the more it becomes evasive. However, if the person says "It will come back to me, I'm sure," and temporarily does another question, the first answer will simply surface out of nowhere and show in the conscious mind.

The key to maintaining a good memory is always affirm your ability to remember. And when the answer does come, simply say: *"Thank you, I appreciate that."* We will have more to say on the *"Thank you"* words later. They are powerful!

SELF MASTERY THROUGH SEDLF-TALK

In 1922 Emile Coué's book *Self Mastery Through Conscious Autosuggestion* was published in the United States and it is still available through many book dealers. In it he explains how the system works and presents plenty of examples of its use on clients.

He also came up with some interesting quotes, one of which is: *"Do not spend your time in thinking of illness you might have, for if you have no real ones you will create artificial ones."*

We mentioned this earlier. If you think or fear you have an illness, it may well occur simply through thinking about it. For instance, a person who frequently makes such a seemingly innocent remark as "Arthritis runs through our family," they are unwittingly setting themselves up through negative imagery.

The lesson here is: "Think well and Be Well." In fact Coué in another quote says: *"Every one of our thoughts, good or bad, becomes concrete, materializes, and becomes in short, a reality."*

Coué's classic suggestion which can apply to any condition for anybody is: *"Day by day, in every way, I am getting better and better."* It is still very much in use today all over the world, but when Coué stepped off the ship at New York to make his first visit to the United States, the news media ridiculed his work and also his classic, all-embracing auto-suggestion.

Coué became known as the Father of Auto-Suggestion and the Guru of Self-Talk. When he died in 1926 his methods were being copied by many teachers in the United States and auto-suggestion eventually created an industry – a New Look at Self -- with such people as Norman Vincent Peale, W. Clement Stone, Robert Shuler and Shad Helmstetter. Shad created a veritable gold mine of usuable auto-suggestions in the classic book *The Self-Talk Solution.*

SOME EASY SELF-TALKS TO REMEMBER

If you suffer from stress and its affiliated symptoms such as mind-chatter, inability to have a good night's sleep, suffering from *"taking work home"* with you, or failing to think well of yourself, here are some suggestions you might adopt for use in your Sanctuary of the Mind.

I find it easy to relax and let go of the tension.

Relaxation is important to my body, mine and spirit and I always get the right amount.

As soon as my head touches the pillow, I let go of all thoughts and tensions, and slip off into a deep healthy sleep. It's all right to sleep deeply.

I am a unique human being. There is no other person quite like me. That makes me unique.

I let go of stress by conscious relaxation and plan my future, which includes good, healthy exercise.

I gain a healthy level of strength every day by going to my Sanctuary of the Mind.

I enjoy exercising because it moves my energy and keeps me healthy.

When I leave my office, I close the door and always leave my work there.

I practice living in the Here and Now. I am a Now person.

You would be surprised at how many people, particularly in health administration, social services and law enforcement take their work home with them and allow it to influence, even seriously disrupt their home life including good sleeping habits.

CREATING YOUR OWN SELF-TALK

In your Sanctuary of the Mind when you are completely relaxed, review your current life. What are the critical stress points you need to address? Impatience? Lack of time for exercise? Lack of sleep? Overeating? Headaches? A suffering relationship? Others?

Mentally make notes and do this without judgment, comment or opinion. Look at each problem objectively, and when you feel you have adequately reviewed your situation, come back to full waking consciousness.

Then spend a quiet evening with pen/pencil and paper, and write down some auto-suggestions. If you feel you lack the creativity for this, go on line to a search engine and put in the words "self-talk suggestions" and a whole flood of different websites offering auto-suggestions will come up. You will even find a page of them at my website www.robert-egby.com.

BE POSITIVE, THINK POSITIVELY

Whatever you do, make absolutely sure that each auto-suggestion is positive. Example: *"The pain in my back is going away,"* is totally negative and reinforces the condition. Here's something more positive: *"Every day and every way my back is feeling stronger and better."*

If you need the help of a health professional, someone experienced in self-talk, give them a call. Most hypnosis counselors are experienced in auto-suggestion. You will find them in local directories. You will be glad you did.

When you have a developed and honed a list of pertinent auto-suggestions,pick two or three and return to your Sanctuary of the Mind. As you relax mentally or vocally say each one slowly and deliberately and with the desire to achieve. Never chant mechanically. Each word has a value and should be recognized.

Remember Jon, the lean, beady-eyed, unshaven, disheveled fellow who started this chapter? He had so many problems that I actually sat down in my audio-room and made him a double-sided thirty minute audiotape which he could play in his car as he drove to work every day. It was non-relaxing and loaded with auto-suggestions for his relaxation and wellbeing. It covered all aspects of life.

Three months later he came back into the office. "He was a different man, very well presented. "Robert, you won't believe this. Last night my dog chewed your tape to pieces. It was a wonderful tape. Give me another. Please!"

CHANGING YOUR EMPLOYER

Most of our problems in life exist from the way we "see" or think of things. Some time ago I wrote an article with the head: *"Don't Change Your Job, Change Your Boss."*

It happened because a young woman named Linda came by, stressed and out of sorts. *"I have a job which I like, it pays well, but I just can't stand the boss. He's egotistical and a bully. I wish he'd drop off a cliff."*

"Why don't you change your employer?" I asked, *"but before you do that, get rid of the thought that you'd like your boss to drop off a cliff. You would feel really guilty if he did just that."*

"Well, I don't wish him any harm," Linda snapped hastily. *"He's just a bully, but I don't want to change my work there because the job is good. It pays well."*

"Why don't you work for the Universe?"

"Huh?" Her stare was frozen in time.

"Work for the Universe," I said with a smile. *"First, tell me what you do?"*

41

"I handle incoming orders from customers, discover exactly what they want, tell them when their orders can be delivered," she said. *"All told I handle some fifty orders a day and I answer scores of queries. I keep busy."*

"Think of that. *It demonstrates that you're helping a lot of people in the course of your day,"* I said. *"So all you need to do is change your boss without pushing him off a cliff."*

Linda relaxed and grinned. *"So what's this Universe business?"*

I explained that the Universe is an energy force. Some people call it Cosmic Consciousness. The good thing about it is that the cosmos is totally impartial. It does not hold grudges and has no egotistical inclinations to bully.

I continued: *"You help a lot of people in the course of your life, so just change your way of thinking. Tell yourself: I work for the Universe! Write it on a card where you can see it at home. Keep a copy in your desk drawer."*

"Just like that?" she laughed with a quizzical frown.

I nodded. *"An old Hindu teacher I met many years ago, told me that if I work for the Universe, the Universe will always repay me. I've always remembered that."*

"Do you work for the Universe?

"Absolutely!"

And it's true, no matter who you are, breadmaker, drycleaner, taxi driver, clerk, waiter, manager, small business owner, author, journalist, even the CEO of a major company, look beyond the process that hands you a check each week or month. If you are helping people, anywhere on the planet, you are working for the Universe, and the Universe will repay you—it always does. It is one of those Natural Laws.

Resist the temptation to figure out how the Universe will repay you, simply allow it to happen. You will know when it happens, and do not forget to say "Thank You," and get on with your life.

Linda came by some months later. "That bully boss has gone. He didn't fall of a cliff but he was transferred to a branch in Wyoming. The new guy is a charmer and I'm now a supervisor," she declared. "But I really like working for the Universe. It sure is different and enlightening."

MOVING ALONG THE HEALING PATHS

So far we have dealt with straight relaxation in altered states and healing that can be accomplished with imagery along with your objectives, desires and passion. Up to now we have dealt with the personal healing path. It is something you can do in your own home without the assistance of a healer, whether it is a dedicated and certified healer in a church, or a health professional.

In reality, you are your own healer. This depends upon your desire, enthusiasm and discipline. Healing is achievable. There is another important factor, the belief in a Higher Power.

You do not have to believe in God or the Universal Mind as I call the Force, or Infinite Intelligence as the Spiritualists say, or even believe in spirit doctors and spirit healers, but it does help.

Bishop John Shelby Spong said in his weekly Q&A Newsletter (January 28, 2010): *"When I speak about God I embrace the fact that I am only using words as symbols that describe not God, but my experience of God. I experience God as the source of life, the source of love and the ground of being."*

Whatever experience you have of God, use it in your life and for healing.

Personal healing is simply a correction or a realignment of bodily energies. Each one of us has the ability, the inner power to make healing happen. And it happens all the time. In fact everything written so far in this book, allows the seeker of healing to perform the function for himself or herself.

Even an atheist can heal. Doctors and surgeons do not heal. They prepare the way for healing to commence. It is a built-in faculty that comes with your human body.

However, it does help, and it has been scientifically proven that if you believe in a higher power, God, the Universal Mind, Infinite Intelligence, Allah, Yahweh, Holy Spirit, your healing will be accelerated. It has also been shown by various studies, that if you are relaxed and feel good about yourself, the body's abilities to heal are accelerated.

Prayer, that much orally abused function, is a wonderful tool. It's the gateway to the Higher Self and the Universal Mind. It will get things done but you have to take responsibility and do your part, otherwise it may not work.

THE SPIRIT BEHIND THE HEALING

It's a common and unfortunate trend among a lot of spiritualists and spiritually minded folk to declare: *"I believe in Spirit. Spirit knows what is wrong with me and Spirit will heal me."* That is very effective, if you believe as the Teacher said: *"God is Spirit."*(John 4:24)

Some Spiritualists have a classic: *"I leave all healing up to my spirit guides. They know best."*

That's like the story of the man who went swimming and got caught in a rip-tide, lost energy battling the currents and started to drown. A lifeguard came up. *"I'm here to save you."* The swimmer called out: *"God will save me. God will save me."* The lifeguard retreated. Next came a crew in a rescue-boat. *"God will save me. God will save me,"* cried the swimmer. The last rescuers came in a helicopter which hovered over the swimmer. *"God will help me. God will help me."* Those were his last words.

When the disillusioned swimmer reached Heaven he stormed up to God. *"What happened? I believed in you. I told everybody you would save me."*

God shrugged. *"Hey, swimmer, I sent you a lifeguard, a rescue boat and a rescue helicopter. Why didn't you take my help?"*

It's the same with healing. When we are sick and need healing, each one of us has to acknowledge (1) we have the ability to heal, and (2) we accept help from whatever quarter it comes. If you leave it up to God, the Universal Mind and fail to do your part, you may end up, like the swimmer, complaining to the Creator.

As we delve into Healing Paths, some of the modalities we explore may well exist in the outer limits beyond your current beliefs. As the Galilean teacher said long ago: *"If you will make room for it in your mind..."* In another words, if it will help you heal, go for it.

Countless people have lost their lives because of their belief systems and this will become evident as we walk the healing paths described in ensuing chapters. Perhaps your beliefs will be challenged in the upcoming chapters, Something that may help: Write down the following auto-suggestion and stick it on your wall because it may well be your finest tool for healing, your lifeboat, your helicopter: *"I keep an open mind and I explore all paths open to me."*

5

ESCAPE TO A NEW LIFE

HAVING AN OPEN MIND is not easy. Chances are, your ego – the False Self – does not like the concept. It's Future! The ego detests the future. The False Self lives, thrives on and manipulates memories. It is an echo of the Past.

Ever since we were born, we have lived in a world that suggests we can improve our basic happiness by investing in things that are "approved of." Such as having an approved of career, marrying the "right" person, having a residence that announces "success," and acquiring friends and associates "who matter."

We build castles on foundations of sand, and somehow they get washed away along with our basic happiness. We have this urge to find happiness in exterior things, and frequently we find that what we have been struggling to achieve is just an illusion. We have lost control. It's a picture painted on water that shimmers and moves to another dimension.

We live in a rapidly changing illusion. Nothing is what it seems. Life, education, careers, marriage, families, relationships, technologies, science, medicine, investments, all are illusions based upon what someone said they should be.

When the illusions start to crumble, what happens? We suffer. We get angry, jealous, fearful, helpless, bitter, tense, confused, and more. Suffering and its brothers, stress and anxiety, eat at our very immune systems. We cannot think straight, and our health and well-being suffer.

As I explained in detail in my first book *Cracking the Glass Darkly,* ever since birth our subconscious minds have been trained, influenced and molded by events in our environments. There was no fixed agenda, no curriculum, no manual, it just happened. Emotional events in the home, along the street, at school, college, work, relationships, all contributed to the education of the subconscious mind which, because it came into the world empty, absorbed everything like a hungry sponge. Everything was sucked in.

ECHOES OF THE PAST

I once asked a group of mothers, how many found themselves talking and acting to their children in ways their mothers had talked to them. In spite of the passing years, most of them acknowledged they heard their mothers' voices coming over loud and clear in their own lives. All echoes from a distant past.

The subconscious mind creates an ego, an image that we think represents us. It is an illusion, but because we believe it is true, it plagues and haunts us for most of our lives. Even though it is crippling our lives, our health, our relationships, our careers, we have impression it cannot be changed. The good news is that it can be changed, and you have the power.

The ego is known as the False Self because it is made up of false images, false impressions, much like a mosaic, full of bits and pieces. The False Self is made up of "faces" or masks very much like an actor playing masquerades. The actor keeps on changing the masks or faces depending upon the emotion, the character he or she is forced to portray. I use the word "force" because the ego is a manipulator, and as such is often called the *"devil within"*. It only exists in our lives when we are awake.

Remember the time when something went wrong in your life, something very embarrassing, and you wished the ground had swallowed you up. Think back and see if you recall the different faces of the false self that your ego displayed. Perhaps initial surprise, then shock, a red faced, denial, a fabricated explanation to fit the situation, then excuses, argument, anger and resentment that your excuses were not accepted, and so on. And then when it was all over, feelings of guilt or embarrassment set in. These were all faces of the False Self. If this ever happened to you, did you manage to watch yourself? Impartially, without judgment, without comment?

If you had, the whole event would have started to take on a different mode, a different experience. It's called the Light of Awareness.

THE FACES OF THE FALSE SELF

The False Self is made up of hundreds, perhaps thousands of faces. Some of the dominant ones include: **anger, jealousy, posturing, helplessness, rejection, envy, discontent, despair, anguish, deviousness, lying, worry, fear, panic, rage, criticism, bitterness, revenge, boredom, limited thinking, tension, foolishness, confusion, flattery, conceit, ignorance, insecurity, obsession, possession, self-condemnation, terror and hatred.**

When a person allows any number of these "faces" of the False Self to run rampant in their lives, it can be costly. Relationships, careers, social standings, and of course health, all can be impacted. The False Self will undermine life, take a person into depression, reduce the immune system, create a failing health and bring about death. It was not so many years ago that many famous men died in "duels of honor" over some-times ridiculous situations brought upon them by the ego or the False Self. And of course, countries have gone to war because of the inflated egos of their leaders.

THE TRUE SELF WITHIN

The opposite of the False Self is the True Self, otherwise known as the Overself. Some people refer to it as the Spirit within. It is a center of unconditional love, a power that exists in all men and women. It is the reflection of the Creator, the God-Force that exists in all of us. It is that part of you that radiates love and it exists within everyone.

When a person says "I don't love myself" you are listening to the voice of the False Self. Ironically, on the physical plain we glibly talk of love. For example the love a man has for a woman, a person's love of golf, movies, football, skiing, bowling. It might be a love of work, ambitions, achievements, success. A love of books. This is the Universal law of attraction working. Each one is limited. It suits the ego, the False Self because each "love" consoles a memory in the past. It's an attraction that passes. It is finite.

Why? Because frequently it is centered on pure self-interest. In a word it is selfish. It gives only as long as it gets. *"If you love me, you'll do it"* and *"I love you so you're mine,"* and *"We are soul mates. That means you have to love me."*

True love is infinite. True Love is the domain of the True Self. True Love does not change because the one who is loved has changed, perhaps through hurts, perhaps through aging, perhaps through an attraction to other energies. True love is unconditional. It is eternal. Infinite. True love does not judge. It is rooted in deep compassion and reflects beauty, perfection and heals without thought and consideration.

True love for which humankind is searching does exist, but it fails to exist where one wants to find it. It's like a human treasure hunt. People are searching frantically all over the Planet hoping to find that true love. The great teachers have proclaimed all along that one has to *"look within"* to find the Holy Grail, the place Jesus the teacher described as the Kingdom of Heaven.

THE CAPTIVE SELF

It is there, deep inside you. The problem is the True Self, the Overself, the spirit that is the Creator, is held in captivity. It is enclosed and shackled behind psychological bars, a psychic prison, and the warden is the False Self. The True Self is imprisoned and in many cases cannot manifest or express itself in one's life.

St. Paul put it so well in 1 Corinthians 13: *"When I was a child, I spoke as a child, I understood as a child, I thought as a child: but when I became a man, I put away childish things. For now we see through a glass, darkly;"*

The glass darkly is the False Self, the negative ego, the prison, the curse of humankind. It causes much of the humanity's suffering. Lao Tzu, Gautama Buddha, Zoroaster, Plato, Jesus, they all saw it clearly and all said you can be saved from suffering, if you would only allow yourself to see it.

THERE IS A WAY OUT

There's one thing that terrifies the False Self and that is awareness. The ego cannot stand the light of awareness. When illuminated by an impartial consciousness, it starts to lose power, it shrivels up, it disintegrates. The False Self is like a criminal, it enjoys the safety of working in darkness. A criminal detests exposure to the light. So does the False Self.

If you really want to test this theory, the next time someone in your life demonstrates anger, stay cool, and ask in a quiet but firm voice: *"Have you ever watched yourself when you're angry?"*

Chances are you will witness some rapid face changing of the False Self. Why? Because you have shone the light of awareness on the face of anger.

So how do we discover the way out? First of all, we learn to resist judging. We live in a world that promotes and basks in making judgments. We frequently judge others, but it is even more intense when we judge ourselves. The False Self loves judging and will seemingly fight to the death to reserve its right to judge.

One of the catches in judging others is that it sets up the law by which we judge ourselves. For instance, if we see some young people in town with purple hair and it reminds us of the so-called dark side, we announce to our friends and colleagues that *"Purple hair is monstrous. It's the color of witches and demons."* Repeated enough, it becomes ingrained. Then, one day it comes back like a painful boomerang when our teenage daughter comes home with the latest hairstyle – purple!

EXERCISE: THE KEY TO ESCAPE

This is not a meditation, so find yourself seated in a comfortable chair. Close your eyes, and imagine, just imagine that you are outside your body, looking back at yourself. Imagine you can review your entire body. Take your time. Slowly and systematically scan yourself from your feet all the way up to the top of your head. How do your shoes and feet appear? Your legs. Your clothes. Review the body inside the clothes. Are there any stress points? Old hurts?

While you are doing this, resist the urge to judge or comment on what you are doing and observing. Do it without comment, without opinion, without expressing any views at all.

Your False Self may well come up with such comments as: *"This is a waste of time,"* or *"This is totally foolish. I don't believe this."* You may well be surprised by the reactions the False Self tosses at you. Simply observe them without judgment. Persevere and when you have finished the scan, take a deep breath and as you breathe out, open your eyes.

Welcome to Impartial Self Observation! This is an ancient practice handed down from the Aryans, the first settlers in India. The name Arya in Sanskrit refers to an individual of higher consciousness. It is said they were the survivors of ancient Atlantis. Their teachings were carried into Persia by the Sufis, the mystics of Islam. The practice was later studied by George I. Gurdjieff, a Greek-Armenian mystic who lived among the Sufis for some 15 years, before bringing the teachings to Paris and the western hemisphere a century ago.

PRACTICE OBSERVING YOURSELF

Perform the above exercise several times until you get used to observing yourself impartially. Then, from time to time, observe yourself, just a minute here, a minute there while you are performing simple and routine functions around your home and environment. Such as cleaning your teeth, writing a letter, cooking a meal, walking along the street, gardening, even meditating. In other words, performing actions where there is little emotional and distractive activity.

When you feel confident, move on to stage two. Remember to observe yourself when you are a little upset, slightly annoyed or impatient and perhaps anxious. Do this without judgment, just observe your feelings and movements. Observe how the feelings of the False Self dissolve when illuminated by awareness.

READY FOR THE BIG TEST

There will come a time when someone says something that really pushes those old response buttons. The False Self wants you to flash the faces of annoyance, irritation, nervouseness and even anger. This is where Impartial Self Observation comes to the rescue. Do it almost as a habit, without judgment, without comment, without opinion, and note what happens to your emotions. If you have become skilled in the practice, the annoyances will start to diminish, and all you have done is to observe yourself.

Keep practicing. There will come a day when your False Self returns to its old self and puts on some hard, nasty faces – like anger, jealousy, rage, obsession, depending on your ego state. Take a deep breath and slip into your Impartial Self Observation mode. Watch those faces of the False Self, without judgment. The first time, they may struggle before they diminish, but as you progress, you will find the faces getting smaller and smaller, and the accompanying suffering diminishing.

As this happens, a change comes over you. The True Self, the Inner Self, the Higher Self starts to manifest its influence. There will come a time when you recognize something. Freedom! You may declare triumphantly: *"Wow. I've broken free!"* Beware of jubilation. Observe your reaction. Is it the truth or is it the old False Self falsely jubilant in your new found abilities? Observe the jubilation and check if they are echoes of your old False Self. If you see the truth, allow yourself a smile and move on.

YOU HAVE CHANGED!

This is healing in progress. This ancient technique is one of the healthiest exercises that anyone can adopt. Impartial Self Observation opens the gates, it allows the True Self to break through the chains of negative behavior, the glass darkly, and flood your mind and body with infinite love, the love of the Creator, the Universal Mind. The Great Spirit.

There will be shocks and bumps along the path. People will still attemp to push your buttons, but you will meet them with self-awareness.

They will never be able to hurt you the way they did in the past. What is more, you will not hurt others the way you did in the past.

When you fail to live and react in the "old way," people, particularly those close to you, will cry out: *"You've changed. You're not the way you used to be. We don't like that."* When you hear such cries, you will understand that that is their own False Selves reacting. Regard them with compassion, love and understanding. Know that in all of this, you have altered your energy vibrations. You have moved up a couple of knotches. If your friends and loved ones ask for your help, explain it to them but do it with care. If they reject your offering, smile and walk on your own way. Your energy will attract similar pilgrims with matching energy and philosophies along the way.

WHY THE FALSE SELF MUST DIE

A healer who walks the Healing Paths of the radical spiritualist has no option but to dissolve, delete, and "kill" the False Self. Failure to do so, undermines the entire spiritual process. A spiritual pilgrim must dump the False Self early in his or her healing quest, discard it like an old cloak or jacket in a garbage dump.

And whether one appreciates it or not, a true healer must work with energy from the Universal Mind, the God-Force, the Creator. To attempt to be a healer within the shadow of the False Self is to work in self-deceit. The False Self will falsely claim that it can performing the healing.

The solution? Get out of your own way, These six words apply to healers, mediums, leaders of spiritual groups, and teachers and pastors of churches and spiritual organizations.

Mystic philosopher and teacher, Paul Brunton in his book *The Ego: From Birth to Rebirth* wrote: *"The danger of most pseudo-spiritual paths is that they stimulate the ego, whereas the authentic path will suffocate it."*

It a tragic fact of life that many spiritualist churches, spiritual organizations, clubs and societies, and recently home churches have fallen by the wayside because the leader or leaders have been engaged in power struggles, wanting events to go "my way," and refusing to see the writing on the wall, the destructive faces of the own ego.

It is sad to relate that a short half century ago there were hundreds of spiritualist churches scattered across the United States, many attempting to perform valuable work.

One common fault was the *"Eternity View."* This is when a pastor saw himself or herself as the sole leader, and did not have the insight to train successors. When the pastor passed on through old age or retired through sickness, there was no one to carry the leadership banner, and the spiritual center succumbed to history and the dusts of time.

Luckily, there are spiritualist churches where pastors have initiated and encouraged training programs for ministers, mediums and healers. When you see a church newsletter containing a listed team of ministers, mediums and healers, it is a healthy sign that leadership is spiritually dedicated.

THE IMPORTANCE OF HERE AND NOW

Incidentally, when you perform Impartial Self Observation, it may well dawn on your conscious mind that you are living in the Here and Now. You cannot live in the past with this awareness exercise, and the future is out too. Observing yourself impartially can only be done in the present moment, the Here and Now.

In recent times there has been a flock of books on living in the Here and Now and while people read the books, go to workshops, and listen to lectures, few people seem to benefit from living in the present.

Jane told me: *"It's like meditation, I can't do that either. I've always had a problem doing anything new. Is it like doing nothing? Wasting time? My mom balls me out for wasting time."* Jane's False Self was having a field day defending its status.

"What are you thinking about right now?"

"Huh?" The question seemed to distract her. *"Oh, nothing, really."* She laughed quickly.

"Really, Buddhist monks spend years developing the art of thinking of nothing. So what are you thinking right now?"

"My boy-friend dumped me last night. My mom got angry."

"So you are suffering right now?"

"Am I not supposed to suffer? My mom says it's all my fault."

"Do you love this young man?"

"We were friends. Good friends. We dated a lot," she said. *"But it hurts. Rejection really hurts."*

Jane went through my list of "faces" of the False Self list, and picked out 'rejection' and 'anger' and 'revenge'."

I had her imagine her suffering as a form. She said it was a big red blob, with a rough coat, and very cold. I had her imagine she was putting it on the table.

Then she placed her hands on her lap, feet flat on the floor and focused on her breathing which initially was shallow and fast. I took her through the Yogi Complete Breath which is deep breathing, then I asked her to describe how she was feeling in different parts of her body. "My back feels better since we started," she said. "It's not so tight."

How is your body feeling, sitting in the chair?

Jane started to describe in detail how she was sitting. *"I'm feeling more relaxed, than when I came in."* At my request she went on to give a running commentary on what she saw in my office, and even included the sun shining on the busy street below.

So what have you doing, I asked.

Jane described how she had learned the Yogi Complete Breath and then how she described herself sitting in the chair, my office and the street scene outside.

"Now, where is the cold red blob on the table?"

Jane laughed. *"Funny, I don't see it. It's not there. Why is that?"*

"Because suffering is all in the past. It cannot exist in the Here and Now," I told her. *"Right now, we are together, you and me. There is no other time, no other place. There is just presence. When you learn to live in the Now, there are no thoughts of yesterday, no thoughts of tomorrow. You simply enjoy and experience living in the Here and Now."*

"Will my suffering return?"

"If you allow it. If you identify with it. But you can let it go and be free by living in the Now. As you walk down the stairs be conscious of yourself walking. As you get into your car and start the engine, be totally aware of

what you are doing. As you drive along the street, be totally conscious of what is happening around you. If you stop for a coffee be there, with that coffee, nowhere else. Enjoy the coffee. Keep practicing, and you will find things of the past will stay in the past, and you will be free of suffering."

"Do you mean I should ignore the past? Forget it?"

"Not at all. It is always a matter of choice. Learn from the past, plan for the future but always live in the Here and Now. That releases a person from all suffering.

I wish those great spiritual leaders could have recognized women a little more. So I have done it for them: I have a (modified) quote by Gautama Buddha said: *"To enjoy good health, to bring true happiness to one's family, to bring peace to all, one must first discipline and control one's own mind. If a man (or a woman) can control his or her mind he/she can find the way to Enlightenment, and all wisdom and virtue will naturally come to him or her."* The emphasis is always on the person, you, the one seeking healing or using healing powers.

6

IN THE PATHS OF THE MASTERS

YOU MAY ENJOY the idea of a "miracle," and if it warms your heart, that's fine. Miracles are simply events beyond our understanding, beyond our comprehension. The more you walk the Healing Paths the more you will come to understand and welcome the love and warmth of "events beyond our understanding," and accept them for what they are.

One day, as our higher awareness expands, we will comprehend, but this will not alter the fact that there is an ability, a gift, a process that enables negative energy in all living things to be restored to a positive condition.

HEALING BY THE GREAT TEACHERS

Jesus, the great Galilean teacher and healer was gifted with the ability and used it well in various ways.

In the case of the nobleman's son at Capernaum, the healing was done by remote suggestion and nothing else: *"You may go. Your son will live."* (John 4:50). Another technique used by Jesus was direct suggestion. It happened at the pool at Bethesda. A man crippled for 38 years was unable to get to the pool. Jesus told him: *"Get up. Pick up your mat and walk."* At once the man was cured, picked up his mat and walked. (John 5)

Suggestion is powerful. You do not have to say what it is for. One must presume that in the following case, Jesus gave a mental suggestion. It happened in the case of the man with the withered hand. Jesus simply told him *"Stretch out your hand,"* and as the man did so, he was healed. (Luke 6:10) In the case of the blind man at Jerusalem, he spat on the ground and made clay of the spittle with which he then anointed the eyes of the blind man. He then instructed the man to go and bathe in a pool. The man did so, and received his sight. (John 9)

There is an even more dramatic case at Bethsaida (Mark 8:22) of a blind man being healed. Taking the blind man by the hand, the Healer brought him out of the village; and after spitting on his eyes and laying His hands on him, asked simply: *"Do you see anything?"* And the man looked up and said, *"I see men, for I see them like trees, walking around."* Then again Jesus laid His hands on the man's eyes; and looked intently and sight was restored. The man began to see everything clearly. Here was a treatment using saliva and the laying on of hands.

There was the case of two blind men and Jesus asked if they believed he could heal them, and they responded in the affirmative. Then he touched their eyes and told them *"According to your faith it will be done to you,"* and as he spoke, their sight was restored. Then he warned them sternly, *"See that no one knows about this."* Well, they promptly went out and spread the news throughout the region.

Jesus warned people not to do this many times, yet they could not resist publicizing his works, which of course, along with performing miracles on the Sabbath, added to his demise on Calvary.

The healings conducted by Jesus are among the thirty-five so-called miracles listed in the Bible, but there are several references to the fact he performed many more healings that were never recorded. For instance Matthew notes: *"There came great multitudes, bringing the lame, blind, dumb, maimed, and many others, and cast them down at his feet and he healed them."* (Matthew 15:30-31) Were these healings en masse? It appears so and maybe we shall never know the full story.

BUDDHA'S MANY MIRACLES

In the eleven major religions of the world, Jesus was not the only originator to perform miracles. Buddha is reported to have crossed the Ganges instantly without a boat, and fed 500 disciples without previous supplies.

He healed a sick woman simply by looking at her. The 50-volume *Sacred Books of the East,* edited by F. Max Muller at the turn of the 20th century reports that Buddha *"converted multitudes by his many miracles."*

Zoroaster who founded Zoroastrianism in Persia (now Iran) performed no miracles in the earliest documents, but later documents showed the *"curing of diseases, counteraction of wolves and other noxious creatures, liberating of rain, confining of hail, spiders, locusts and other terrors."*

Zoroaster's teachings had more impact on the Old Testament than any other religion. Kings of Persia are mentioned in eight books of the Old Testament, and the first book of the New Testament describes the very first visitors to the new-born Jesus were wise men from the East, the Magi, identified as priests and astrologers of Zoroastrianism.

Muhammed, according to Robert Ernest Hume in *The World's Living Religions* quotes the ancient Mahomedan writer Mirkhoud who said that the originator of Islam repeatedly disclaimed miracle-working powers, although he was challenged to do so, and later is reported to have *"wrought many miracles."*

The early Christian fathers practiced spiritual healing in much the same way as taught by the teacher, Jesus, although as the years passed, so-called pagan practices were introduced with the use of spells, herbs and sorcery. For many years oracles were a great form of healing for the general populace.

HEALING, A PAGAN PRACTICE

Constantine, the founder of the Universal (Catholic) church triggered end empowered the early church to fight against pagan practices, and it was not until half a century later that Emperor Theodosius came along and banned all pagan worship and healing, destroyed temples, oracles and soothsayers and made Nicene Christianity the only permissible religion of the empire. His infamous edict issued in 380 A.D. triggered a saga of religious intolerance, widespread violence, torture, executions and murders which lasted for centuries. Christian heretics were shown no mercy. Even healers were banned for associating with sick people. Let's face it, who else would healers associate with? It is the dark side of

Christianity, an aspect which continues to prompt the faithful to criticize and undermine spirit communication and Spiritualism as a religion or a practice even today.

Through the so-called "Dark Ages" that followed the collapse of the Roman Empire in the Fourth Century A.D to about 1000 A.D., baths, pools and holy spas came into prominence, but they were not promoted for fear of being termed paganistic. They formed a "healing underground."

Healing in the churches remained in the dark for many centuries. It was not until February 11th 1858 when a 14-year-old peasant girl Bernadette Soubirous admitted to her mother that she had seen a "lady" in the cave of Massabielle. People believed the vision to have been of the Virgin Mary, and suddenly, Lourdes in France became a point of pilgrimage for thousands who wished to be healed. Pope Pius IX authorized the veneration of the Virgin Mary in Lourdes in 1862.

The Bernadette vision came ten years after the advent of Modern Spiritualism at Hydesville in 1848, so students of history can well appreciate the intense reaction of the mainline churches in that decade.

THE DIVINE TOUCH

The laying on of hands came to be known as the "Divine Touch" in the later ages. The kings and queens of England and France possessed it. Edward the Confessor, (1003-1066) one of the last Anglo-Saxon kings of England had it as did most of the monarchs. Queen Anne who died in 1714 was the last to claim the divine practice. The French kings performed their divine abilities up until the French Revolution started in 1879.

HEALING BECOMES LEGALIZED

It's worthy to note that the healing practice among the peasantry flourished in the towns and villages of England through the Middle Ages. There were clairvoyant-healers, soothsayers, sorcerers and witches. If you needed to have a limb removed, you dropped by the local barber who performed the task with saws and knives. They later became known as "barber-surgeons."

The sixteenth and seventeenth century saw some interesting developments that shook the local healing practitioners. In Edinburgh, Scotland on July 1st 1505 the barber-surgeons were incorporated as a Craft Guild and their charter gave them some exclusive powers in healing. In essence freelance surgery was banned. Similar organizations followed in Scotland and England, and in 1681 King Charles II granted an all-empowering charter to the Royal College of Physicians of Edinburgh.

The local healing fraternities found themselves closed down and any form of healing, psychically or otherwise became illegal. Apothecaries, who had prescribed herbs and various concoctions were incorporated into the various guilds and suddenly the ordinary folk of Britain—the peasants—discovered they could not afford the escalating fees of the incorporated barber-surgeons and the physicians. The result? Riots ensued in many towns and villages.

This was just sixteen years after the Great Plague struck the British Isles and many families were still recovering. King Charles is reported to have asked the newly growing organized medical fraternities to ease off persecuting local healers, but the seeds of power had been sown and are still prevalent today.

In spite of the fact that their acknowledged founder, Jesus made healing a key part of his ministry, the mainline Christian churches appear to have lost the gentle art of hands-on healing or anything resembling it. Early Spiritualists in the late 19th century adopted a laying-on of hands healing as a recognized function of the Spiritualist religion. This, as we shall see, still exists today.

And as I write this, I find there are growing voices in the Christian wilderness. A Presbyterian minister fought the resistance held by many in the church that the idea of touch-healing was tainted with suggestions of intimacy, sexuality, and power. He sought for answers, including the study of bodywork and healing in China, Thailand and Hawaii. Eventually he graduated from a massage school where he had learned body awareness. He went on to sharpen his pastoral skills and then teach the practice of touch healing.

The minister's name is Zach Thomas and his book *Healing Touch: The Church's Forgotten Language* provides real insights into bringing back healing into the 21st century mainline churches. Today, he is a certified bodywork therapist and minister in Charlotte, North Carolina. He is founder and president of the National Association of Bodyworkers in Religious Service. One message that comes over for would-be healers is *"become educated."*

HEALING PHENOMENA AT SCOLE, ENGLAND

At a senior citizens community, I finished giving a talk on healing and a sharp faced little lady accosted me: "I really don't see how you people can do healing. Only Jesus knew how do it."

It's amazing how many people can read with awe and wonder of the healing phenomena described in the Bible, and yet question or outright reject healing in modern times. It's almost as if such phenomena is not supposed to happen today, yet the energy and the Cosmic powers are available in modern times as they were in days gone by.

In the mid-1990s a number of healings took place during a five-year investigation into human interaction with paranormal phenomena.

It happened at the tiny village of Scole in Norfolk, England. The team comprised four people known as the Scole Experimental Group. They were Robin and Sandra Foy and two mediums, Alan and Diana Bennett. The mediums would go into trance and convey messages from a team of spirit communicators on the Other Side. It started on a weekly basis and the sessions, quickly observed by noted scientists and researchers produced some incredible phenomena.

For instance, films never used in a camera, were placed on the table during a spirit session. When processed the films showed handwriting, hieroglyphs, various symbols and messages. Grant and Jane Solomon's fascinating and very readable book *The Scole Experiment: Scientific Evidence for Life After Death* should be required study for all Spiritualists. Recently another book, detailing each of the many sessions in logbook format has been produced by Robin Foy. Entitled Witnessing the Impossible it reports on each session from December 20th 1993 to the final, rather dramatic sitting on November 6th 1998 when the Experiment was closed down. It also lists the 180 phenomena that occurred.

HEALING AT SCOLE

Healing took place at the Scole sittings. On Sunday, August 25th 1996 Tina Laurent was one of nine people invited to sit in with the group. She later wrote an article which was published in the *Spiritual Scientist*. In spite of an "irritating, tickling cough" she attended the circle and afterwards declared it to be *"the most memorable day in my life."*

In the article Ms. Laurent tells how a *"spirit light"* impressed the group with its movements and dancing ability. It then approached her, hovered gently in front of her face, and she gave it permission to enter.

"It immediately whooshed into my solar plexus area, making a small plop as it entered my body (felt, not heard). It moved around for a little while, giving me a tingling sensation (like a bee trapped inside my jumper) and then moved quickly down my arm and plopped back into the room through the back of my hand."

Ms. Laurent concluded: *"What do I make of this? Well, I know that the love encountered in the cellar that afternoon was very real and tangible, and, surprise, surprise. I haven't coughed since then!"*

We live in an age where people like to attribute a healing to the healer, or in the Scole case, a dancing Spirit light. Let us make one thing clear: Healing in a recipient, whether it is a human being, an animal or a tree or a plant, only occurs through the power of God, Infinite intelligence, Universal Mind. A healer is a conduit. A spirit healer is a conduit. They relay healing energy to the person or subjects in need of healing.

HANDS-ON HEALING WORKS

Hands-on healing for the most part works, providing you have the right connections, the power of the Universal Mind. If you visit a spiritualist church or a spiritualist home circle where part of the service is hands-on healing, you will see healers routinely conducting healing. Some carry National Spiritualist Association of Churches (NSAC) certification, while others are simply healers who work for the love of healing. We call it Divine Healing.

Chances are most people can be healed and most people can give healing. You may have given unwittingly. This is the sharing of inherent healing energy.

For instance, healthy mothers heal all the time while they are bringing up youngsters. A child hurts himself or herself, and mother takes the child in her arms, talks lovingly and caresses which is great, but she is also enveloping the little one in her own energy. Her own energy brings the child's energy into her auric field and they vibrate together.

It happens with adults being among adults. A person is hurting over an injury or the loss of a loved one, and an empathetic adult moves into the sufferer's energy field. There is an immediate change as the two energies merge, and the stronger one dominates and starts the healing process. For a simple one-on-one healing that's fine.

But if you're a healer, or training to be a healer, and you believe you have the ability to heal others all by yourself, watch out. Your resident energy will not be sufficient and you may tire easily and become ineffective. A good healer becomes attuned and relies on Cosmic energy, the Universal Mind, God, whatever. When you wish to pursue the noble art or the gift of healing, use Cosmic energy which comes in abundance and never withers or wears out. What is more important, if the recipient wants it, it works very well. Good healers often work with spirit guides or angels, and we will deal with that aspect later.

EXERCISE: ALIGNING COSMIC ENERGY

It's not easy to tune into Infinite Intelligence, the Universal Mind, Holy Spirit, unless you build up a little self-confidence and have dumped the False Self. These tried and true techniques will get you into the mindset.

(1) Relax and slip into an altered state of consciousness as described earlier. When you feel comfortable, place a coin - a quarter will do - in the center of your palm, and gaze at it intently. Imagine, just imagine that it is getting warm. Feel it getting comfortably hot, then let it stay there while you count slowly up to ten. Then

let go. Breathe in and as you breathe out, say "Wide awake. Wide awake." Practice this exercise until you feel comfortable.

(2) Next, return to an altered state of consciousness again. When you feel comfortable hold your hands unclenched in front of you, palms facing each other, about six to eight inches apart. Close your eyes and then say quietly: *"Holy Spirit, I attune my body, mind and spirit to the Universal Mind and I ask that I be allowed to channel healing energy for the good of all people, including myself. Amen."* Then wait a few moments and sense your hands becoming warmer. Enjoy the experience, and after a minute or so, thank the Universal Mind, and make yourself "Wide awake." You are now ready to study hands-on healing, traditional Spiritualist style.

THE SPIRITUALIST HEALING TOUCH

One fascinating phenomenon that occurs in Spiritualism is Spirit Healing otherwise known as Hands-On Healing or the Healing Touch. Follow the instructions below, and you will find you can perform elementary spiritual healing. I say *"elementary"* because there are some protocols, as we shall see.

The actual touch is important in healing. It helps to have a few other things such as: (1) Feeling good about yourself; (2) Do healing with enthusiasm or passion (passion is the energy for getting things done); and (3) Possessing a belief or knowledge that there is an Infinite Intelligence that empowers the Universe with life.

A healer, in addition to healing the mind from the False Self, should maintain a clean body, taking a shower before conducting a healing anywhere with any person. It helps for the healer to meditate, and build up Cosmic or Psychic energy as described in the Healing Tree in the Sanctuary of the Mind.

Then you need to relax. If you have been practicing the early instructions on getting into a light trance, it should be easy. Now, find someone who needs healing and is likely to give you objective, unbiased and useful feedback.

EXERCISE: THE HANDS-ON TECHNIQUE

Find a quiet, comfortable place where you are not likely to be disturbed. Turn off any electronic communications devices. Arrange some soft lights. You might like to have some soft, easy-on-the-ear music playing. Music is important as we will recognize in sound healing. Burn some easy incense like sandalwood, and perhaps a candle. Be careful of having too many candles. I once knew a healer who almost asphyxiated someone seeking healing. She had at least fifteen candles burning in a small healing room, and wondered why patients complained of a lack of air.

Have the person wishing healing (the healee) to be seated in an upright chair. The back of the chair should be low enough for you to access their neck and shoulders. The healee should sit comfortably, no slouching, legs side by side, and hands resting easily on the thighs. It is good for the healee to close his or her eyes, as it reduces possible visual distractions.

Stand behind the healee, take several slow deep breaths, and adopt an attitude of faith that there is in the Universe an Intelligence that will provide you with all the healing energy necessary to achieve your goals.

A PRAYER FOR HEALING

Feel or sense yourself being attuned to the Universal Mind. Incidentally God knows what you are doing. If it helps, say a prayer, something like: "Holy Spirit, I am sustained by Living Spirit. If it be thy will, allow the healing power of the Universe to flow through me now to heal (Name the Healee). Allow the healing, to flow through my body and hands with Love, Harmony and Peace." If you wish to create your own prayer to the Universal Mind, that is even better. God does not get bored, humans do.

Some healers spout off a lot of fancy and flowery words designed to impress. Long time healers cut to the chase and say something like: *"Holy Spirit, allow me to be a channel for your healing for (Name the Healee). Amen."* Jesus the healer in Matthew 6:5-8 says do not be like the hypocrites, pray quietly, *"for your Father knows what you need before you ask him."* In this case, healing.

Next place your hands lightly on the shoulders of the healee. Your thumbs should almost meet at the top of the spine or base of the neck, and spread out across the tops of the trapezius muscles or shoulders. Be confident that you are a channel for healing energy.

If you are clairvoyant and clairsentient you may sense a beautiful, beam of pure white healing energy coming down from up above, and flowing through the crown of your head to your shoulders and down through your arms to your hands.

Do not be alarmed if your hands suddenly feel hot and tingly, like it did with the coin exercise. It occurs and may be much more powerful. This demonstrates the energy is moving. It may feel hot or cold, or you may not feel it at all. But the recipient will. It's one of the peculiarities of healing -- the energy will always fit the healee's requirements. After you have been an instrument of healing for a while, you may no longer feel the energy, but the recipient will. They may well exclaim: "Oh, your hands feel so warm."

THE WAY OF CONTACT HEALERS

Hands-on healers are often called contact healers. They may place one hand upon the recipient's forehead and another upon the back of the neck. Contact with the head and shoulders is sufficient for the purpose of healing by beginners. Touching the healee in any other place on their body is unnecessary, and if the person is a stranger, even someone outside your family, charges of unprofessional conduct may result from doing so. (This is why I go along with Zach Thomas's advice to get educated and become a professional body-worker if you wish to practice healing anywhere. Professionalism removes or should remove doubts in the healee's mind of your integrity.)

Healing energy flows. Spiritualists believe that once the energy is inside the human body it is directed to the areas that require healing. Accept what healing there is, normally powerful stuff.

Healing, particularly for a serious condition, will require several sessions. How long is a session? In a church healing, four or five minutes at most. In private practice they can run for five, ten, fifteen, even twenty minutes. You will know when it's over, because the energy will stop flowing.

CLOSING THE HEALING

When you have finished, mentally thank whoever you pray to, then move to the front of the healee and imagine you are closing off their body from any negative exposure. You do this by gently moving your open right hand in a clockwise circle over the solar plexus, and saying: "I am now closing you off." This brings the solar plexus chakra back to normal. During healing, the solar plexus chakra often assumes an "open" state, and if left in that condition, the healee will walk around picking up all sorts of feelings and emotions from other people.

As you progress in this beautiful work, you may sense other spirits working with you. They will be spirit guides, spirit doctors working from the Other Side. But always remember it is Infinite Intelligence, God, the Universal Mind who is the source of all healing energy.

Never administer Hands-On healing in place of treatment by a professional health office or physician. Ensure the healee understands this.

If you wish to pursue spiritual or hands-on healing, training is available. Contact your local Spiritualist Church. There are, of course, various healing books available at the bookstores. Books such as *Spirit Healing* by the great British healer Harry Edwards make good reading for the would-be hands-on healer. Incidentally, most church-based spiritual hands-on or contact healers do not charge for healing. The National Spiritualist Association of Churches has a prayer which is heard in most churches and among Spiritualist groups.

THE PRAYER FOR SPIRITUAL HEALING

I ask the Great Unseen Healing Force to remove all obstructions from my mind and body and to restore me to perfect health.

I ask this in all sincerity and honesty and I will do my part.

I ask this Great Unseen Healing Force to help both present and absent ones who are in need of help and to restore them to perfect health.

I put my trust in the love and power of God.

SOME THOUGHTS AND OBSERVATIONS

Some healers work alone while others have a helper, a spirit guide from the Other Side. Mine is Chang, he's been with me for many years. The last time he walked the physical Earth was in the 1890s when he served as a doctor in a remote province of northern China.

This is why, perhaps, I am inclined to be very conscious of bodily and cosmic energies, the yin and the yang, which according to philosophy, are complementary opposites within a greater whole. You cannot have a yin without a yang. You cannot have light without darkness, male without female, high without low. You cannot have sound without silence. Everything in the Cosmos has both yin and yang aspects, which constantly interact with each other, never existing in absolute states.

RESTORING THE YIN AND YANG

Spiritual healing, contact healing or laying-on of hands is a beautiful and natural healing process that restores the yin and the yang. When spirit doctors work through a healer their energies bring the patient's energies back into balance, the yin is balanced proportionately with the yang. Pain and sickness are alleviated for the person on Earth being healed.

While hands-on healing is painless, many people find it very uplifting and providing a sense of inner awareness. It is difficult, if not impossible to say it will work, so there is no guarantee that a healing will be accomplished quickly. Some people being healed break into tears as stressors and perhaps hidden memories surface and are expended.

Spiritual healing is normally permanent, however, there are exceptions and they rest with the patient. People who have received spiritual healing should maintain basic rules of health and well-being. That is cleanliness, good eating habits and plenty of rest. The renewal of strength and the beginning of healing starts with the patient. Right thinking and right action are good healthy policies.

WHY SOME HEALINGS FAIL

There are many reasons why a healings fail. For example, the patient continues to break the rules of good health that brought about the illness in the first place, or there might be psychological-mental reasons why healing is being blocked, and thus appears to fail. Spiritual healing may well reduce or eliminate "mental blocks," or if the blocks are too deep and intense, the healee may need to seek qualified professional counseling.

Simply put, if you pursue the habits or activities that triggered the condition in the first place, and after healing, continue with those negative habits or activities, chances are the condition will return. You are responsible for yourself.

In Vancouver, British Columbia, the old Vancouver Psychic Society would hold special healing services one Sunday a month and the Society's healers would work on dozens of people. I recall working on twelve in a two hour period.

LILY FROM THE LAUNDRY

One heavily built English woman named Lily came in every month with the same complaint – rheumatism, pain and stiffness accompanied by swelling in her legs, particularly her knees.

"When I have healing I leave feeling I can run a mile. My old knees feel like new," Lily told me. *"But it doesn't last. It gradually comes back."*

Curiosity got the better of me. I needed to know what she was doing. *"We run a laundry washing hospital sheets and stuff, and I often have to get down on my hands and knees and clean the machines,"* she said sadly. It sounded like something out of a Charles Dickens novel. I told her if she wanted the healing to last, she had to find some way to get off her knees. Incredibly, she had failed to make a connection between her damp work and her rheumatism.

Lily did not appear at the Sunday healing services for two months, then one day I met her on Granville Street, her face was all smiles. "We now have a young woman cleaning the machines," she cried happily. "My legs are feeling better with the passing of each day."

IT'S ALL IN THE TRAINING

Thinking back to Lily, the method of laying-on of hands in those times differed greatly from what happens in Spiritualist churches today.

The person who trained us as spiritual healers was Isabel Corlett who founded the Vancouver Psychic Society. An Isle of Man native, she came to Canada via London where she had sat, learned and observed with such notable Spiritualists as Maurice Barbanell, Air Chief Marshal Lord Hugh Dowding, Ursula Roberts, and of course, the great Harry Edwards who founded the Spritual Healing Sanctuary at Burrows Lea, Shere in the Surrey countryside in 1947. Harry's healing attracted thousands from all over the world, and when he crossed into spirit in 1976, his work at Shere was carried on for many years by Ray and Joan Branch.

Harry Edwards wrote in his classic book *Spirit Healing* that every healing is an individually planned act, performed by an individual spirit guide to meet the specific needs of the sufferer within the law. This, he said forms the logical basis on which every healing is accomplished.

Harry Edwards, Isabel Corlett and many like them, worked with sufferers in an open style that became classically traditional. With the person's verbal permission, they did hands-on healing in a multitude of ways, resting their healing hands on various parts of the body—legs, feet, stomach, chest, back, arms, hands, head, face—and sometimes wrapping their arms around the healee in a bear-hug. It was positive healing directed and aided by spirit and, it worked!

TRADITIONAL HEALING CRIPPLED

Ironically, modern times and modern thought have crippled valuable and effective spiritual healing styles in the churches. In recent years a number of alternative healing movements, particularly massage therapists have come into prominence and state and local government legislators have enacted stiff rules and regulations on what constitutes a massage therapist.

A Spiritualist healer in church, working on a sufferer and moving his hands over swollen joints and muscles could find himself or herself contravening laws that totally govern another modality such as Massage Therapy.

To avoid such conflict, the National Spiritualist Association of Churches issued instructions that all healers must be aware of state laws and abide by rules for healing set by their churches. State, county and municipal laws can change from place to place.

Example, in Connecticut a healer can place hands on the healee's shoulders and then hold the hands of that person.. In Massachusetts the healer is restricted to placing hands on shoulders and head only. In New York the healer can place hands on the body. Some churches say nowhere down the front of the body (neck to thighs) male or female. In some states you cannot touch a person's hands, the healer resting hands only on the shoulders. Because governing statutes are so changeable from place to place, at National Spiritualist conventions healers are instructed to conduct healing through the laying-on of hands on the shoulders only.

The irony of all this is none of these restrictive statutes points the finger at Spritualism or church healing. And churches or church organization never lobby or express opposition and concerns over legislation which may effect their religious healing practices.

Spiritualism is a registered religion in the United States and has been since the late 19th century. It is an affront to that religion to allow traditional Spiritualist healing to be manipulated, influenced and even curtailed by laws designed for other healing modalities.

If they had truly valued and strongly believed in traditional healing techniques, the various Spiritualist organizations, should have long ago, decided to make their views known to the lawmakers in various states, and openly fought for their rights in religious activities.

EXPAND FIELDS OF HEALING AND AWARENESS.

Most Spiritualist Churches feature a hands-on healing service lasting fifteen to thirty minutes attached to the weekly devotional services. Most services are on Sundays, but there is a growing number with mid-week services that include healing.

Many churches have classes specifically designed for healer training. One is the Plymouth Spiritualist Church in Rochester, NY where training includes: Guided Meditations to Meet Healing Spirit Guides, Creative Visualizations, Body, Mind and Spirit Connection, Working and Practicing with Raising Vibrations & Moving Energy, Aura, Colors, Sound, and Understanding Natural Laws.

One Spiritualist group – don't call it a church -- that can be said is breaking traditional boundaries is the relatively new Celebrate Life Spiritual Community in San Francisco, California. As I write they are teaching Qi Gong which is an ancient mind-body Chinese discipline that cultivates the Qi, the life force energy in the body. It is considered to be the foundation of Chinese Medicine and Acupuncture. This static meditation technique helps students to clear energy blockages along the invisible pathways, called meridians. In addition to the above, this Spiritual Community is expanding its outreach into different communities that is likely to make traditional Spiritualist pew-sitters cringe.

Celebrate Lifers make trips and donate food and clothing to various orphanages, conduct sacred-concerts at which healing takes place, donate to the Aids Lifecycle event, and among other activities, sponsor an orphan for a full year of secondary education, including room and board. This is radical spiritualism coming on strong. You can find out more about this Spiritualist Community at www.ourcelebration.org.

THE SCIENCE OF SPIRITUALIST HEALING

No one seems to be able to put a finger on when the Spiritualist movement got around to being like Jesus and healing people with just a touch. But Spiritualists have also claimed that Spiritualism is a Science because it *"proves"* things like communicating with departed loved ones and spirit teachers in the Other World.

If you are seeking certification as a healer, you must have written evidence that the healing you gave to someone in your church actually worked. They are called affidavits and "prove" that you have given healing. The problem is, that once you are certified, the scientific mode ends.

Few if any healers actually keep records of the healee's state of return to health. They may keep unusual anecdotes resulting from healing accomplishments for use in talks, articles and books, but otherwise there is little scientific proof that healing took place. In other words where is the scientific evidence that healing works?

DISCOVER WHO YOU ARE HEALING

Lily, the lady we mentioned earlier, was an exercise in learning. It was from her that I found out that one should take time out to listen to those seeking healing. In other words conduct a pre-healing consultation.

This is difficult in a church environment where people seeking healing, simply approach the healer, sit in the chair, and receive healing. They come, they receive and they disappear. You might refer to this as *Blind Healing* but traditional Spiritualists will respond with *"Spirit knows what the healee requires."* Blind healing puts the onus on God, Infinite Intelligence, the Creator, which to some extent is fine if you really do not wish to know or prove whether the healing is effective. In the old traditional healing process this is acceptable, if you are a traditionalist.

However the Radical Spiritualist, particularly if he or she works in or understands another healing modality, will ask a lot of questions and form a profile before giving healing. People seeking healing are only too willing to talk about their plights and it pays to know who you are healing.

This raises the question: Should people attending a church for healing, meet with the healer in advance of the service, and discuss the healee's condition? It is at that point that records could be kept and the healer could conduct follow-ups for the record. This process would help to give stature to the "science" of Spiritualism.

THE NEED TO COMMUNICATE

When we lived in Westville, New Jersey, a young man I had seen receiving healing in the Spiritualist Church there, came to my office for a professional consultation. For several minutes he beat around the bush, and then when I pressed him, he exclaimed: *"I went to the church for healing. It worked for a few days, then it comes back."*

"What comes back?"

"My upper chest pain. It hurts when I breathe," he said quickly, rattling like a machine gun spouting bullets. *"People don't understand. I'm gay. I have AIDS. I think I'm going to die."*

"What does your doctor say?

"Never go to doctors."

On my desk is a list of phone numbers of key resources in the area. All therapists in any modality keep them, or should do. I wrote down the name of a lady doctor nearby. *"She's one of us. She'll check you out. Then come back and let me know how you get on,"* I said. *"And you're not going to die, at least not for a long time."*

"How do you know?"

"I'm psychic," I said with a short laugh.

A week later he returned for a healing imagery session. *"Your friend sorted me out. I'm on anti-biotics for chronic bronchitis. She said if I had let it go, it could have been pneumonia."*

He paused while sitting in the hypnotherapy recliner.

"So tell me, how did you know?

"Your spirit guide, the angel who looks after you told me. His name is Henry. Has an English accent, a Jordie from Newcastle."

"That's my uncle! He's been gone twenty years. I lived with him when I was a kid!

"Well," I said with a shrug. *"He wants you to know you need a kick up the backside. Whatever that means."*

"That's Uncle Henry! Always said that."

"And he's still saying it, so I want you to close your eyes and just imagine...just imagine you are in a Special Place...with nothing to do, nothing to think about...just to relax. I'm going to give you suggestions for living.."

7

THE HANDS OF LIGHT

RELIGION AS WE KNOW IT seems to put a time-lock on people, cultures and many civilizations in general. To break the chains of the time-lock, one may well suffer the indignity of being called a heretic, an atheist or something that the tide washed up. There are clerics on television expounding threats of hellfire and brimstone gathered from a book that was designed for desert tribes and fishermen two and three millennia ago. One wonders why any logical thinker would want to be imprisoned in a time-lock.

Jesus was a great healer and sage who lived in Galillee. His fabulous Sermon on the Mount reflected teachings of the ages, teachings that many Christians (and clerics) cannot find it within themselves to even follow. When one views the pomposity of the Vatican attire that reflects neither the time of Jesus nor the twenty-first century, one wonders in what time-lock they may be living?

Here in upstate New York I regularly watch the Amish with their quaint black buggies, relics of another age, living and dressed in a long-ago time-lock as they mingle with speeding bundles of metals, plastics and rubber held together by high technology and called autos. One wonders again, why the time-lock?

And then we have the Spiritualists with their ages-old style of hands-on healing, a blind modality that assigns responsibility to Spirit.. One wonders why the time lock? Did not Jesus look to a variety of methods for His healing?

It was inevitable that sooner or later, someone would come up with an organized, far-reaching, scientifically trackable method of the old hands-on healing of the Spiritualists. Like many other religious movements, Spiritualists are not enthusiastic about evolution which may place them in a time-lock as well.

A BREAK INTO A NEW WAY

It happened in 1972. Dolores Krieger, an RN and professor of nursing at New York University, and Dora Kunz, a psychic healer who had been involved in Theosophy discovered and implemented it. They called it Therapeutic Touch or TT as it is now known.

It occurred in a moment of desperation a year earlier. Ms. Krieger was tending one of her patients, a hospitalized 30-year-old woman who was steadily dying from a gallbladder condition. Frustrated with what was happening, Dolores tried a hands-on healing technique she was learning from Dora Kunz. After one treatment, a positive response occurred. The patient lived, and surprised everyone including hospital staff..

Krieger and Kunz met a Hungarian hands-on healer named Oskar Estebany, who was fast becoming a world renowned healer. At Canada's McGill University he had successfully performed non-touch healing by holding the cages of wounded mice. He retarded the growth of goiters in mice suffering from iodine restricted diets. He also demonstrated that healing energy could enhance plant growth.

A THREE YEAR STUDY GROUP

Kreiger and Kunz invited Estebany to form a three-year study group and observed his work with patients. Estebany practiced healing on various patients using the laying-on of hands.

Kunz, using her own psychic and intuitive abilities would observe and assist in the healing. Krieger scientifically recorded everything that happened with profiles of the patients. The couple learned that the energy transfer between the healer and the patient is Prana, a Hindu word that means energy, vitality and vigor. Prana is in the air that we breathe as will be discussed later. It was from all of this that Krieger and Kunz developed a modern, clinical version of hands-on healing, otherwise known as Therapeutic Touch. .

From the very beginning it scored a high rate of success in bringing about rapid relaxation, reduction of pain and discomforts, accelerated healing, and resolving psychosomatic conditions. It is reported to have been successful in the relief of nausea, diarrhea, migraine, fever, joint and tissue swelling, measles, asthma and many more.

WORLD-WIDE FOLLOWING

Originally developed for use by health professionals, it quickly became so popular and in demand, that now, almost four decades later, well over 150,000 people around the world have been trained in TT, about half of them healthcare professionals. Many of the health care professionals use TT as an aid to traditional medicine. Practitioners in osteopathic, naturopathic, chiropractic and homeopathic therapies are also reported to use Therapeutic Touch.

Dolores Krieger in her 1997 book *Therapeutic Touch Inner Workbook* describes Therapeutic Touch as a contemporary interpretation of several ancient healing practices that are concerned with the vital-energy field of the human body. She says the therapist acts as a *"human support system guiding and repatterning the healee's weakened and disrupted vital-energy flow."* The result is that the healee's own immunological system is stimulated and recovery is strengthened and reinforced.

Practitioners are taught to enter an altered state of meditation or "centering" as TT puts it. In addition they are taught intuitive skills and how to be sensitive to changes in the chakras, the human energy wheels, and also changes in the vital-energy.

"Touch" is central to TT and the practitioner's hands may either rest upon the healee's body to read energy information, or float several inches above the body sensing energy changes. The reason for this, says Ms. Krieger, is that instruments to reliably measure the matrix for vital energies have yet to be invented.

Therapeutic Touch sessions generally last about twenty to thirty minutes. During the various programmed steps, the healer places the palms of his or her hands two to three inches from the patient's body and sweeps them over the energy field in slow, gentle strokes beginning at the head and moving down the body to the feet. The practitioner is aware of such phenomena as heat, cold, pressures, heaviness, or other sensations such as tingling. Cues translate into signal blockages or disturbances that need to be addressed. There are five distinct stages in the practice.

Practitioners are advised to always use energies in a constructive manner and warned not to fall into the maws of the four terrible dragons of self-delusion, the enemies of Therapeutic Touch. They are: fantasy, exaggeration, impulse and wishful thinking.

Therapeutic Touch is now practiced in over seventy countries worldwide in hospitals, clinics and nurse training institutes. It is taught at over 100 universities and medical schools around the United States and Canada. Although TT was developed primarily for nurses and health professionals, anyone can learn and use it. Most hospitals do not charge extra for TT assistance.

It seems that whatever affliction it is applied to, Therapeutic Touch has a positive effect. The interesting aspect is that while it is based on the use of Prana, the all-powerful Cosmic and Universal energy, it is not tied to religion, yet it is esoteric. The beauty of this modality is that the energy goes right to the target, the area where it's needed. It rebalances the human body, and brings all cells back into alignment.

Incidentally, Dolores Krieger has written several other books over the years and they are in print. Two we enjoy are *Therapeutic Touch: How To Use Your Hands To Help or To Heal,* and *Accepting Your Power to Heal: The Personal Practice of Therapeutic Touch*

EXERCISE: TOUCHING THE ENERGY

While the experts say the best way to learn TT is in a class, this technique will give a student a sense of the bio-energetic field.

Sit comfortably with both feet on the ground, bring your hands together until the palms are about a quarter to half an inch apart. Feel the energy growing, and as you do, slowly draw your hands apart until they are two inches apart.

Now, slowly come back to the starting position, and again draw them apart until the gap is about four inches. Keep doing this action, drawing the palms further apart until they are some eight or nine inches apart.

Slowly bring your hands together again and you will feel a cushion of energy existing between your hands, like an invisible cushiony ball. Check it for resistance and elasticity. Also make a note of any bounciness, resistance, elasticity or sensations such as heat, cold, tingling or pulsations. This gives you a sense of the bio-energetic field.

If, at this point, you wish to hold your hands over someone's body, you may bring about a pleasant form of relaxation, and perhaps induce some other benefits. For the serious radical spiritualist who wishes to get into scientifically based esoteric healing and become certified, TT is a good opportunity. Go to your favorite search engine and put in the words: "*classes for Therapuetic Touch*" Chances are there will be some near you.

8

PAST LIVES:
A FORCE FOR HEALING

SOME PEOPLE CALL IT PRE-EXISTENCE, others transmigration, palingenisis and others call it metempsychosis. American and British Spiritualists know it as that perennial thorny issue – reincarnation. Spiritism, the sister of Spiritualism, created by Frenchman Allan Kardec in the mid-19th century, not only teaches a belief in spirits and communicating with spirits of loved ones and ascended beings, they also teach reincarnation. Officially Modern Spiritualism does not.

According to a twenty-two page report, dated December 9th 2009, and issued by the Pew Research Center's Forum on Religious and Public Life, 24% of the public believe in reincarnation. There's more: 25% of Catholics believe, and 25% of people who are not affiliated with any particular religion also believe.

While Modern Spiritualism officially refuses to acknowledge past lives in any form, many spiritualists do believe in reincarnation and discuss it openly in workshops and forums. Because of this presence of an ongoing interest, the subject is quite often raised at annual conventions of the National Spiritualists Association of Churches.

But the Association is in alignment with the orthodox Christian churches who are tied to actions taken almost 15 centuries ago at Constantinople. An important church council (Universal Catholic) anethamatized – that is cursed – the doctrine of pre-existence of the soul.

This, in spite of the fact that in the Old Testament God told Jeremiah: "Before I formed you in the womb I knew you, before you were born I set you apart; I appointed you as a prophet to the nations." (Jeremiah 1:5 NIV)

The ancient church while banning the doctrine of pre-existence, completely overlooked the fact that if you ban the doctrine of pre-existence, you also eliminate transmigration, otherwise known as reincarnation. The early Church fathers in attempting to kill a sparrow, shot off their own foot.

Two-thirds of the world's population which is now close to seven billion, believes in reincarnation, but this is not the purpose of this book to substantiate the belief. We leave that to academics such as the late Dr. Ian Stevenson, the Canadian professor of psychiatry at the University of Virginia who spent forty years studying 3,000 childhood cases suggesting past lives.

Science is gradually over-shadowing New Age practitioners in the Past Lives regression business. Clinical psychologist Allan Botkin while counseling Vietnam veterans in a Chicago area VA hospital accidentally discovered IADC, that's Induced After-Death Communication during therapy sessions with a vet named Sam. During a session, Sam saw a vision of a Vietnamese girl he could not save. She told him everything was okay and she was at peace now.

This single moment surpassed months, even years of therapy and allowed the vet to reconnect with his family. Since that 1995 discovery Botkin has honed the process and used it to treat countless patients. His book *Induced After Death Communication* includes dozens of case examples and this form of therapy has been taught to professionals across the country. Thus science is making healing inroads into a field that was once, in western thinking, New Agey.

PAST LIVES IMPRINTS: FAMOUS CASES

As we explore the Healing Paths of the Radical Spiritualist we find we have a deeper and more humane aspect of looking at past lives. In a nutshell, the healing of past life imprints.

Imprints are memories, experiences, information and knowledge carried sometimes at a conscious level but predominantly at a subconscious level by many people. Imprints can be positive or negative or even mediocre. Positive ones can come in the form of talents and knowledge, such as the ability to play a piano and compose like a master as did four year old Wolfgang Amadeus Mozart in the 18ᵗʰ century.

Then there was Carl Friedrich Gaus of Germany who not only became an outstanding scientist but was billed as the "Prince of Mathematics." At three years of age, he spotted a mistake in his father's business calculations. Then there was Jose Capablanca of Cuba who, at the age of four, beat established adult chess players, and when grown up held the "World Chess Champion" title between 1921 and 1927. His speed of play astounded everyone who watched him.

It is not only males who carry imprints. Giannella de Marco an eight year old Italian girl, conducted the London Philharmonic Orchestra at the famous Royal Albert Hall in London. They played works by Weber, Haydn, Wagner and Beethoven. The Times newspaper reviewer wrote: *"She plies a clear, generous beat and plainly has the music at her fingerends. There is an unnerving maturity in her intellectual accomplishment...."* The London concert was the 123rd of her career which began at just four years of age.

In modern times, there is the case of author Frank de Felitta and his wife Dorothy who suddenly heard their six year old son playing Fats Waller style jazz on a piano keyboard -- a keyboard he had never touched before. A shocked Mr. de Felitta told reporters it was "beyond my comprehension." The experience prompted him to write a novel with a reincarnation theme entitled *Audrey Rose*. The book was later made into a movie with the same name, starring Anthony Hopkins and directed by Robert Wise.

Today, that six year old jazz pianist is Raymond De Felitta, an independent film maker whose work as a writer and director has been honored around the world, including festivals in Cannes, Sundance, Toronto, and more. And yes, he is a life-long jazz pianist producing his own CDs. Check raymonddefelitta.com .

NO RHYME NOR REASON

Frequently, there seems to be no rhyme nor reason for how and when imprints surface. Some imprints may show up as dreams or déjà vu feelings that we have been somewhere before. While other imprints may be of a more traumatic nature such as being burned at the stake during the Spanish Inquisition. Imprints may surface unexpectedly and take their owners by surprise.

Not all imprints carried by people are as pronounced as the ones mentioned above. Sometimes, a past lives imprint takes years to manifest. It is almost as if the spirit/soul sleeps until a certain age, then comes to life in a person, and brings profound changes in that particular life. Imprints may also manifest through a trigger, such as a word, a feeling or even a picture.

ALEX AND THE CHINA CONNECTION

Alex was a tall, wiry student, who enjoyed school, particularly mathematics and geography. He sang in the choir at the local Episcopalian church, helped his father in an auto-repair shop and was supposed to be a good choice for getting married, settling down and having a family. His passion was photography and collecting pictures of lions.

One night when he was twenty-two his mother passed his room and heard a strange voice. Curious, she opened the bedroom door. The bedside light was still on and Alex was fast asleep. She moved closer. Words in a foreign language were coming out of his mouth. Shocked, she called her husband. He taped the sounds on a tape recorder.

The next day, they played the tape it to Alex, who listened with a straight face. Suddenly he smiled. *"That's Chinese...Cantonese...it sounds as if I'm teaching school."* Strangely, he showed no surprise at all, in fact he was vaguely amused by the revelation.

Alex called me early one morning. *"I need to explore my past lives. Something is happening."* He would not tell me what prompted the call. As he relaxed in my therapy recliner going into trance, he casually talked of life in a village somewhere in northern China. His voice tensed.

Suddenly he was in a medical school, training as a doctor. *"Now I'm being told I cannot graduate...they need medical students at the front...there is a war...the Japanese are killing my people."*

I asked him for the name of the place and time.

Alex paused to think for a moment. *"It's the summer of 1937..it's the old town of Wanping...thick walls, like a fortress...Marco Polo...there is a bridge and we are trying to carry out the wounded...so much blood...why do I want to be a doctor..I am nauseous..."*

Alex's body perspired as he related memories of the Sino-Japanese War. He told of how he was wounded in the leg, and returned to graduate as a doctor, only to be wounded again by a stray bullet in the Chinese Civil War of 1945. He recovered and started training medical recruits, but this was short-lived. He died of blood poisoning a few months later.

As we finished the session, Alex sat up. *"That's given me a lot to think about. I've had many dreams with an oriental theme. Now they make sense. I have to go back."*

I looked at him quizzically.

"China," he said. *"I have to go back. There are things to do."*

A year later I received a letter with a China postmark. *"I am now in Beijing teaching English to Chinese business people. Thanks for your help in healing. If you ever come over I'll take you to the Marco Polo Bridge. Now I understand why I always liked lions. The bridge is full of lion statues."*

A SENTENCE OF DEATH

Not all past life readings can be so direct and life- changing as the day we listened to Alex. Some can achieve healing through simple revelation.

For instance, when I first started studying metaphysics and possessed little knowledge about the healing opportunities of past life awareness, I went through a period of choking. It was difficult to swallow. My doctor called it phagophobia. Perhaps there was an element of truth in his quirk: *"It's a message from God to lose weight,"* then he added, *"It'll wear off."* Well, it didn't and I spent the next year eating soups and liquid food, and using my newly acquired meditative techniques to reduce anxiety.

"Experience Your Past Lives" proclaimed the billboard poster announcing a one day workshop. It was my first exposure to this part of metaphysics. It appealed to me. The woman, a Toronto hypnotist, put us all into a trance, and lo, before I knew what was happening, I was sorting books in a bibliothèque, a library in the Latin Quarter of Paris that looked like a converted church.

"Focus on a situation, a problem, an ailment that is bothering you now," said the hypnotist. Immediately the scene changed and I found myself dressed in heavy woolen robes, thick leather sandals that hurt my ankles and feet. Noisy people were bustling everywhere. A stench of many acrid odors hurt my nostrils. Smoke from a charcoal fire, a swarthy, heavily bearded man manipulating a fat pig on a large spit with dripping green fat, permeated everything.

Then I noticed the chains. Rough chains attached to heavy iron collars about my neck, wrists and ankles. Somebody, a nasty man with warts on his nose, screamed in my face. *"By order of Henry the Eighth, by Grace of God, King of England, King of Ireland, King of France, you are found guilty of treason and sedition and hereby sentenced to death..."* The voice babbled on. I gathered it was 1539.

The soldiers did a bad job. They hanged me on an oak tree that graced the corner of the road between Wells and Glastonbury in the County of Somerset, England. They were far from professional, just killers in the name of the king. The iron collar was removed and replaced by a prickly thick rope...and the rope was strangling me...I was choking to death. I tried to scream but there was no air, no voice, no feeling. No nothing.

The hypnotist brought me back to full waking consciousness. *"You were abreacting. Reliving an experience in a past life,"* she explained when I revealed the memory to the people attending the workshop. *"I was a monk,"* I said.

The hypnotist asked: *"Have you had a possible throat condition in this life?"*

I started laughing. Had I had a possible throat condition?!!! My immediate reaction was an inclination to say: *"What a stupid question!"* But politeness reigned and I told the workshop of my phagophobia, my fear of choking. It was strange, because right after that event, my fear disappeared, evaporated, and as I later discovered when studying hypnosis and hypnoanalysis, an abreaction can frequently clear a link to a suppressed memory in this life, or as I discovered, a past life.

Some years later as a practicing accredited hypnoanalyst I treated clients who had absolutely no idea of past lives, in fact, I never mentioned reincarnation in the preliminary consultation. The cases, however, had a mysterious way of coming up all by themselves.

THE CASE OF SYLVIA AND JESSIE

This case involved a young woman in New Jersey who suffered chronic migraines and was forced to stop working as a teacher and stay at home in a darkened room. Her marriage sprawled on the rocks and she was tired of taking pain relievers which made her feel nauseous. Her body weight was steadily in decline. We will call her Sylvia.

She called late one night. *"Can hypnosis help my migraine, because if I don't get relief I'm going to kill myself."* She was worn from battling pain and desperate.

Sylvia arrived next morning, a slight, nicely trimmed woman, very well dressed, her drawn face partially covered by heavy sunglasses and framed by blonde, wispy hair. She was 38 years-old and had suffered migraines for over a decade.

In consultation, her childhood was textbook functional. Great understanding and loving parents who encouraged Sylvia to study, attend church, and explore the world. She casually mentioned a fear of guns. Her father had a German pistol from the war.

In systematic, conscious relaxation her headache intensified, so I brought her back to a light state of altered consciousness, alpha. I then asked her to imagine a box with a lid and a lock, and to place her migraine in it for "safe keeping."

Speed was of the essence, so I used a technique taught by Dave Elman, the acknowledged pioneer in rapid hypnosis and author of the classic book *Hypnotherapy.*

Sylvia seemed happy. In a comfortable Theta State and working on a scale of zero (nothing) to ten (maximum), her migraine came in at a low three and she agreed to establish a mental workplace, her own special place, a sanctuary of the mind. It turned out to be a beautiful garden. She gazed around. There were no "dark spots" which might indicate a problem area.

Next, I asked her to *"Find a round spot on the lawn where the grass is thicker, greener and richer than anywhere else. This is because there are special minerals in the soil and gravity is stronger than anywhere else. The gravity spot is a place for letting go,"* I said, and in her mind she promptly took off her shoes and stood on the spot.

With her migraine still at a low level I then asked her to imagine taking the migraine and holding it in her hands and describe it, perhaps a cube, a ball, a blob, anything. She said it was a big ball – black, rough and very cold.

"Now, at the count of three a word, a phrase, a thought, a person, a feeling, a memory, something connected with that rough, cold black ball will simply spring into your conscious mind " I repeated this three times, then counted – one, two, three.

For several seconds nothing happened. *"What are you thinking?"*

"I'm in a bedroom...it's small, drab, very simple... feels like a hotel. The walls need painting ...a suitcase is on the bed...it's raining outside the window...there's someone with me...a man..I know him...Nathan..he's my husband..." She paused, then added: *"I think he wants to kill me."*

"Why does he want to kill you?"

"I refuse to live on the family farm "

"What's your name?"

"Jessica. People call me Jessie."

"Jessie, do you have a cell phone? Is there a phone in the room?"

Her face frowned. *"Phone? What is a phone?"*

This was the first indication that she was experiencing a past life. *"Can you get out of the room?"*

"No, he's blocking the door. He doesn't want me to leave."

"What is the year?"

A frown slipped across her brow as if the question was silly and nothing to do with her plight.. *"1886. April 1886. Why do you ask?"*

"Where are you? What town are you in?"

"Chicago. I came seeking work. We are both out of work. I left Nathan to find work here, but it's not good...not good. People are on strike. Nathan thinks I have left him for good. He's very angry." She suddenly gasped. *"He's going to shoot me...he's pointing the gun at my face. I cannot bear this..."*

In hypnosis, I asked her to experience everything in black and white, which by eliminating colors, reduces the emotions. *"What are you doing?"* I asked gently.

"I cannot bare to look. I've turned around."

Those were the last words Jessie said in that lifetime. A bullet smashed through the back of her head.

"It's strange, I'm in the room...Is that my body on the bed? Oh, Heavens, my body is on the bed...It's all so strange...Nathan has fled...there's someone else here...a woman...my gran.... Granny Telfor... why? She's dead...I must be dreaming...but she's smiling...and there's Grandpa Joey..."

FORGIVING YOUR OWN MURDER

Gently, I brought Sylvia back to her Sanctuary of the Mind to relax and then mulled over what she had seen.

"Is there anyone in your current life that resembles Nathan?"

"There was. My first husband for two years. He was not a nice man, but he didn't try to kill me. He was killed in an auto accident."

"Let's focus on Nathan. Think about these words. You don't approve of what Nathan did, or even condone what he did, but can you forgive him?" We discussed this question for a few minutes, then she nodded and verbally forgave him for her death in 1886. In reality, by forgiving her murderer she was taking a great weight off her shoulders.

When Sylvia returned to full waking consciousness, she shook her head. *"Wow!" Was that real?"*

There was no way I could answer. *"How do you feel?"*

'The migraine...the migraine has gone. I lost it, somewhere along the way, I lost it. My head feels clear. It's wonderful. What did you do?"

"Nothing. You did it," I said smiling. *"Come back next week."*

A FORCE FOR HEALING

Sylvia returned happy and completely free of the old discomfort. In the next school year she had a new teaching job at her old school and the migraines never returned. Now, was that drama played out in a Chicago hotel in the spring of 1886 real? Perhaps, perhaps not.

In her present life she had never been to Chicago or even thought about it. There were serious labor problems in the city at the time, so who knows? The important thing is that glimpse into a past life, something for which Sylvia possessed no belief at all, had served a purpose. It had given her a healing and a new way of life. This, I think, is the benefit of past life exploration. It can be a force for healing.

THE ART OF REFRAMING A MEMORY

At one point during Sylvia's therapy, I could have used what we call a "Reframing" technique. This is where the client non-judgmentally looks at the memory, and sets up two safe spots. "Safe Spot A" is the beginning of the memory, and "Safe Spot B" sits at the conclusion of the memory. It's like having the client review a film clip, and the markers are safe spots.

The therapist then asks the client to "preserve any learnings" from the memory in a special place in the mind, then totally erase the memory, either by painting over the incident with white or black paint, or deleting it with an "eraser" gun. If the incident/memory lasts only a short while, the client can bring the two posts together and firmly strap them together for complete elimination.

For a major, longer memory spanning several hours one has to consider the point that in matters of the mind, nature abhors a vacuum. If the therapist does not fill it, Nature will. Therefore a new positive memory, loaded with color is created and placed between the two posts.

The following example is for a fully grown woman who discovers through dreams and flash-backs that she had a molestation problem continuing to haunt her.

In hypnosis, she sees herself as a young girl walking upstairs. On the way to her room she is caught by her brother, who drags her into his room and for several hours molests her.

After erasing the memory, the reframing would involve the girl, standing on the bottom step, but suddenly she decides to do something else, like going to town, be anywhere except climbing the stairs. When the new memory is in place, the therapist, perhaps in the following session, would have the client check to see what happened that day. Normally, the old memory of molestation is gone and the new memory is in its place.

UPON REFLECTION

Why didn't we do this in the Jessie/Chicago memory in 1886? There were all sorts of reframing options: a policeman at the door investigating shouting, or Nathan's gun could have misfired, or perhaps in his rage he could have dropped from a heart attack. All these were reframeing possibilities.

In any of these reframe scenarios Jessie could have fled from the room, which means the murder never happened and she continued her life perhaps to old age. But this presents an intriguing problem.

The entity currently known in 1886 as Jessie could have been fated to reincarnate the following month or year, and whoops! There is no spirit to reincarnate because Jessie is still alive and well on Planet Earth. Therefore, a reframe to save Jessie and prolong her life, may have created a time warp in the nature of things that could have reverberated and created serious problems for all sorts of people.

Incidentally, past life healing can be very satisfying, and it's an excellent modality for which a radically minded spiritualist can become involved and certified. For someone who feels there is a past life haunting them with negative imprints, I would suggest you find an experienced health professional trained and believing in such a modality.

A HEALING IN JERUSALEM

One story that blows the mind of a lot of people attending my workshops, concerns a dowser, we'll call him Eric.

Eric was in his late fifties, had sold his store and was now retired. He believed in "some sort of spirit" running the Universe, but added: *"I haven't much time for Jesus or Buddha, that sort of thing."* That was his False Self talking, and was due for a wake-up call.

Eric's problem was his back. *"I wake up at night with tremendous pains running up and down my spine. The doc says there's nothing wrong with me and it's all in my head."* Eric said he had checked his house for geopathic zones, and the place was totally free. I always check this point with clients.

In hypnosis, Eric finds that a "dark place" has manifested in his Sanctuary of the Mind which was normally a sunny garden. Reluctantly, he feels drawn into the "dark place" and finds himself as the captain of a Roman galley normally carrying grain from Mediterranean ports back to Rome.

Eric vividly describes the ship being smashed by a vicious storm while off the coast of Palestine. *"Swimming desperately for the shore, I get struck in the back by a falling mast,"* he said. *"Next thing I know I'm in some hostel where the women are looking after me. I can hardly walk. I spend months recovering."*

"Now I'm in Jerusalem...so many people...they say there's a rabbi healer in the city..named Jesus. My back is killing me. I push through the crowds. I can see him. He's passing by. If only I could talk to him. I lunge out and touch his robe...he turns his head and gazes at me for a second, then he's gone. I stand up. New energy is running up and down my body. I'm healed...I try looking for Him...but he's gone. I wanted to thank him."

Eric brings his mind back to the present, gets off the recliner and stretches his body. "I don't believe it, Robert. It's gone. The affliction I suffered for two years has gone. Completely. Not a tinge of discomfort."

I asked Eric if he recalled the first time he had the discomfort in his back. *"My wife and I had been to Expo 86, the World Fair in Vancouver. It was a hot day, so we sat on an Expo seat...someone said there was a tall ship, a sailing ship coming through...so we jumped up to have a look...and as I stretched to peer over the crowd to have a look at the ship..I saw it and, at that precise moment, my back went out."*

Did Eric really experience being a ship-wrecked captain of a Roman galley seeking healing from Jesus in Jerusalem? I don't know. I don't really care. What did happen is that Eric's chronic pain stopped and left him without a trace during that strange session...and that, for the mind of the radical spiritualist, is healing.

While many people explore past lives for thrills, the study of reincarnation as a healing modality is a powerful tool for the radical spiritualist bent on helping people heal.

Healing is always the bottom line.

9

DOWSING:
THE SWINGING HEALER

T OM PASSEY WAS one of the greatest dowsers one could ever hope to meet. He knew energy, worked with energy and he played it to the hilt. He was president of the Canadian Society of Questers. He was also my friend and colleague.

Quester is the Canadian term for dowser, and Tom was not only a great teacher and lecturer, he had a great personality and a tremendous following of students and admirers. He not only came over as a friendly grandfather, but as an ancient wizard in modern-day clothing. Some people thought of him as a reincarnated Merlin from Athurian times in England. By coincidence, he was born and grew up in Wales.

He had an amazing understanding of energy, and told students attending workshops: *"All disease comes from blocked energy. The worst thing you can have in your body is stagnant energy."* In a healing workshop Tom and I did on Whidbey Island, he looked at a woman seated in the front row and said: *"You have an energy block near the bottom of your spine, and it's been bothering you for months."*

The young woman nodded, and Tom asked her to come forward and sit on his chair. As she sat down, he waved his "wand." Most dowsers use pendulums when working closely on a subject, but Tom had a thin black fly-fishing rod that he carried everywhere. It would "talk" to him, in exactly the same manner as a pendulum talks with yes, no, can't say, don't know. I'll explain those in a moment.

"You spend a lot of time crunched forward in a desk chair that's too tall, and it's impacting your back," he said. Her name was Annie and she nodded vigorously. *"I never thought of it that way,"* she said. *"It will be changed on Monday."*

"Okey doke," Tom said. *"Are you ready to let go of the discomfort* (he never called it pain) *and be well?"*

"Oh, Yes! Yes! Yes!"

He tapped her back with his wand. *"It'll be gone at lunchtime."*

Sure enough, half way through lunch, Annie came rushing up to Tom, her eyes glistening with joy. "You'll never believe this Mr. Passey, it's gone! It's really gone."

MOVING WATER

Tom always enjoyed those moments of pure belief. He enjoyed healing, but he detested water. "It makes me nauseous," he told me, which was ironical because he excelled in energizing and moving water.

A Shuswap Indian complained that his well had gone dry. Friends claimed it was the work of bad spirits. Tom looked down the well for a few minutes, then declared *"There's a nice little vein ten feet away. Will fifty gallons a day be enough?"* The Indian was hesitant to say anything, but finally nodded. Next day the Indian, all excited phoned Tom to tell him his well was full with sweet water.

We were in Salmon Arm attending the Canadian dowsers convention. During a quiet moment, I quizzed Tom on how he got water to divert its course. *"It's in the Bible, Bob. The prophet Job said: Thou shalt also decree a thing, and it shall be established unto thee: and the light shall shine upon thy ways."* (KJV Job 22:28) He smiled softly. *"When you are a dowser and you want to change something, you have to decree it. That's the secret. Remember that."*

"Did you do that with Annie?"

Tom nodded. *"Dowsing is the finding, decreeing is the order to the Cosmos for an action to be carried out. It's the same as ask and you shall receive. How many times does one have to be told."*

100

DOWSING FOR HEALING

Dowsing which is part of the ancient art and science of divining had its origins thousands of years ago. In fact it is safe to say the roots of dowsing are lost in the mists of time.

In the Tassili n'Ajjer caves in south-east Algeria there exist incredible wall paintings of wildlife, but there is also a picture of a dowser, holding a forked branch in his hands, and being watched by tribes people. Carbon dating set the paintings at over 8,000 years old.

Ancient Egyptian temples show pictographs of pharaohs with sticks resembling dowsing rods. They date 2,000 years before BCE. One of the Cairo museums contains pendulums over 1,000 years old.

MOSES USES HIS ROD

Since time immemorial, dowsers have called their divining apparatus "rods." In the famous crossing of the Red (Reed) Sea Moses is instructed to use his rod. It's in Exodus 14:16 *"...lift thou up thy rod, and stretch out thine hand over the sea, and divide it..."* (KJV) That was one occasion. The second comes when the Children of Israel are thirsting in the desert. Moses is again told by God to use his rod and strike a rock. He does so and water pours forth. (Exodus 17:5/6)

Whenever the ancients required something, they simply resorted to their rods or their pendulums. They never lacked for water, never lost their way, and the divining rod always answered their questions. The rod and the pendulum became their personal oracles, and they never left home without them. Recall the words in Psalm 23: *"Thy rod and thy staff shall comfort me."*

Today, many people around the world are using dowsing instruments to tap into their higher consciousness, tap into the Cosmic Mind for answers. The original and most popular use for dowsing rods was to discover water sources. It's also been used to find gold, oil, minerals, lost personal items, lost people, historical and archeological sites and much more. One day I arrived at Vancouver International Airport and failed to remember where I had left my car a week earlier. My pendulum led me right to it.

Dowsing has unlimited possibilities. For instance, with a pendulum you can use it to find directions, ask the time, check the energy of a house or apartment you might be renting or buying, how the weather will be on a certain date in the future, the wisdom of starting a business or economic project, starting an education course and much more.

DOWSE TO CHECK NUTRIENTS

In health and welfare matters, dowsing will reveal the amount of calories on a plate of food, and determine the fat content. You can even check the nutrient content of food, and if you have a list of vitamins and minerals, you can check your own or a friend's vitamin and mineral balance in the body. Obtain a list of vitamins and minerals from your local health store or library, and checking each one, ask your pendulum if your body content is in balance. Another favorite of dowsers is checking the sex of an unborn child.

Using a pendulum you can, with permission, scan a friend's body and determine a past history of surgical operations, bone breakages, organ and gland weaknesses, plus energy blockages that need to be resolved. Arthritis, a stress related disease, has a habit of originating in areas where bone breakages occurred and apparently healed years before. Pendulums are great for tracking body and auric energies. Many naturopaths and other health professionals use pendulums.

In metaphysics there are a number of power centers in the human body. They are known as chakras. As you move along your spiritual path you will likely find some chakras being extremely active and others being sluggish. A pendulum will reveal such imbalances, and we will discuss chakras and rebuilding and enhancing their powers in our section on Sound Healing.

REMOTE DOWSING

One interesting aspect of pendulum dowsing is you do not have to have a person in the room with you, to work on them. They can be in Alice

Springs, Australia or Ishmalia, Egypt. A dowser can read the energy and problems of a person living thousands of miles away.

Remote dowsing applies to anything. There are some dowsers who work for oil and mineral exploration companies assisting them in their work, and by all reports, they are quite successful.

EXERCISE: At a set time, have a friend or relative who lives on the far side of town, or in another county, rest on a bed or sofa in their home and do a body scan from your home or office. Check their chakra power centers, then check for any current energy blocks, stress points, and discomforts.

For this exercise it is good to have an outline of a body on a piece of paper, and if you can, have the power centers indicated. If you wish to be really exact, have three body charts in front of you, chakra, muscular and skeletal. Before you begin, write the name of the person on the top of the paper. This keeps you focused.

Make notes of your findings, and then share them with the target. You may be pleasantly surprised at your findings. You can communicate by phone or email during or after the scan. Set a duration period for the scan.

DOWSING – HOW DOES IT WORK?

The dowsing fraternity has a variety of answers, so the bottom line is no one knows for sure. Some say it is a very fine neuromuscular reaction triggered by the higher self, while others claim it is one's psychic ability, while others say the whole thing works on universal or earth energy. One point is definite: pendulums and dowsing rods do not work by themselves. There must always be a human element.

For my part, I believe dowsing is the manifestation of higher consciousness working in conjunction with the sub-conscious mind. It is the metaphysical part of our being, the intuitive sense, the sixth sense that is in tune with universal consciousness.

USING A PENDULUM

You can use just about anything as a pendulum, as long as it swings. A metal nut, key, nail or bolt tied on the end of a piece of string will do. A ring, a pendant or brooch on a fine chain will do too. Most serious dowsers use crystals, polished stones and small brass knobs that come in various shapes and sizes. It is convenient to have a point at the end.

Some years ago a pendulum maker in Canada used shiny point-22 bullets attached to fine chains. When some non-dowsers, criticized the use of bullets for such a spiritual use, philosophical dowsers would respond: "Bullets can destroy, but when used for dowsing they become symbols for peace and healing." The best pendulums are those that mean something to the user. A pendulum should always feel "right" for you. Ironically, you need to use a pendulum to find that "right" one.

CARING FOR A PENDULUM

Once you have established the right one for yourself, get a soft cloth container and keep it as you would a valuable gift. Do not allow anyone else to use it, no matter if they are the most angelic person in the world. If you think your pendulum might have been exposed to negative energy, place it on a piece of cloth and expose it to sunshine for several days. If you are in a hurry, you can wash it in sea salt water or apple cider vinegar. Both are great for cleaning off unwanted energies. Make sure your pendulum is safe for cleaning. If in doubt, use the sunshine mode.

Most pendulums come in velvet or soft cloth bags, and they should always be kept and carried in a protected place.

HOLDING THE PENDULUM

The most practical way of holding the pendulum's chain is with the forefinger and thumb of your strong hand – that's your writing hand. Some dowsers advise using the weak or non-writing hand. It's whatever works for you.

Let the pendulum hang loosely. Some people fancy longer chains, about twelve inches, others like it to be two or three inches. The shorter the chain or string the faster is the response. There was once a naturopath in West Vancouver whose pendulum chain was about an inch, and it seemed to react at lightning speed. Start with a twelve inch chain and discover your own preferred length.

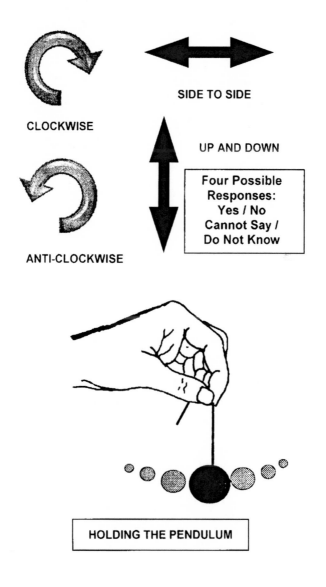

CLOCKWISE

SIDE TO SIDE

ANTI-CLOCKWISE

UP AND DOWN

Four Possible
Responses:
Yes / No
Cannot Say /
Do Not Know

HOLDING THE PENDULUM

THREE OR FOUR RESPONSES

Depending who you ask, there can be either three or four responses obtainable from a swinging pendulum. I teach four responses, my old colleague Tom Passey used to teach three. Again, it is whatever turns you on.

My four responses are: **YES, NO, CAN'T SAY,** and **DON'T KNOW.** The last two responses are based on (1) your higher consciousness refusing to tell you, and (2) the higher consciousness simply does not know the answer.

The first two responses from a pendulum are fairly straight forward. My **YES** is a circular clockwise movement of the pendulum, and the **NO** is an anti-clockwise circle. Yours may be different.

My **CAN'T SAY** is a straight back and forth, and my **DON"T KNOW** is like a shaking of the head, side to side movement. See the attached diagram.

EXERCISE – LEARNING TO SWING

To discover your responses, perform the following exercise. Do it when you are comfortably relaxed. Never hurry when dowsing. It's like meditation so stay cool.

Your arm should be free, not resting on a table or against your body. In fact, many dowsers suggest your arm should be a little tired, much like an arm used in automatic writing. First, give the pendulum a gentle motivating swing then generally keep your hand still after that. Address your pendulum: *"Show me a YES."* This means that when you pose a question to your pendulum, the answer will be in the affirmative.

Now, when you have an affirmative response, bring the pendulum back to a slight swinging mode, and this time ask your pendulum to: *"Show me a NO."*

Next, do as above but address your pendulum as follows: *"Show me the response when you CAN'T SAY the answer a question."*

Finally, ask your pendulum *"Show me a DON'T KNOW response."*

Keep practicing until you get all four responses. They may be weak at first with the pendulum hardly moving, but with practice the responses become stronger. When you feel comfortable with the responses, do this simple test.

A BEGINNER'S QUESTIONS

Prepare your pendulum, allowing it to swing gently in neutral. I normally start a session with *"May I ask a question at this time?"* Some dowsers ask: *"May I? Can ? Should I ask a question?"* It is your choice. Wait for a response and if the pendulum swings an affirmative, perform the following test.

"Is my name......?" Pick the name of someone else. The response should be a negative.

Now use your correct name. The response should be in the affirmative.

Once you have established this, you are ready to go and dowse whatever your heart desires. However, refrain from getting excited, stressed or hurried. Pendulums and your higher consciousness are averse to fluctuating energies. But as Tom Passey advised in countless workshops: *"Practice! Practice! Practice!"* Many people neglect this point. Experience is vital to good, effective dowsing, and experience comes through practice. If you desire to be an accomplished pianist, you must practice. Likewise if you wish to be a good skier, tennis player, mathematician, floral arranger, photographer, psychic and healer, you must practice. So it is with dowsing. Practice at every opportunity you get. Enjoy your trials and errors.

SWINGING IN THE NOW

Whenever you pose a question to your pendulum, ensure you are thinking in the Now. It's important. "Is this educational course right for me Now?" "Is this vitamin right for me now." "Can I use my pendulum Now?"

Pendulums usually go into a "Don't know" response if you ask, "Will I be a success in my life?" Success is ambiguous. It's a subjective, comparative condition.

EXERCISE: FINDING NUMBERS

Sooner or later in Dowsing work, you will need to find a number. The way to go is with the elimination technique, which is as follows. Obtain a jar containing marbles, jelly beans, pushpins, beads, whatever. Your assignment: find out how many items are in the jar.

To use a pendulum for finding numbers, it requires you to ask a series of questions. Let us say the answer is 103 jelly beans. You may ask are there more than 100? Yes! More than 200? No! Less than 150? Yes! Less than 110! Yes. So you know the answer is between 100 and 110.With a practical margin, ask the pendulum to show you a "yes" when you say the right number with a count from 101 to 109. It will swing to a "Yes" when you say 103.

When you need to quantify anything concerning numbers, use your pendulum with the elimination technique. It may sound laborious at first, but with experience the end result comes quite quickly.

You can find out many things this way. I was once sitting in a circle at Port Coquitlam in Canada, and a mother and her adult daughter were sitting opposite me. "The daughter said: "I'd like to know my mother's age?"

I did the elimination technique and my pendulum came back with "Fifty-one."

The mother snapped back. "Thanks a lot! I never told my daughter my age. Now you've blown it." Everyone laughed, and finally the mother joined in.

There's a lesson here. Be careful when intruding on people's privacy, they can get quite hostile. It's unfortunate, that when you think about it, there is nothing, absolutely nothing that is private in the Universe. It's just that some people in our culture like to think there is such a thing as privacy. Sometimes you have to respect people's illusions.

TELLING THE TIME WITHOUT A WATCH

Another great exercise using the elimination technique is telling the time. Always remember to use the words "here and now" with time.

Another opportunity is checking what date your first crocus will bloom, or working out the weather for a particular future event. This is great for people planning major functions such as weddings and family reunions. Hint: If you do work on the weather for a particular function, get another dowser to work with you. That's like insurance.

IS THE PENDULUM ALWAYS RIGHT?

No, but it is nine times out of ten. The time that it is wrong may well hinge on how you posed the question. If in doubt, rephrase the question and see if the response changes.

One last thing with pendulums: It does help to get into an altered state of consciousness, before using the pendulum or doing any dowsing and divining. One simple, easy way is to close your eyes and look up into the inside of your forehead for a few seconds, then open your eyes. That action alone puts you into an alpha state. Enjoy!

Y-RODS AND L-RODS

If you would like to get more involved in dowsing, there are a number of instruments or tools you may wish to learn about and use. The American Society of Dowsers (www.dowsers.org) has a bookstore where there is a great variety of L-rods, Y-rods, bobbers and bounce rods and even the famous Cameron aurameter, and there are articles on how to use them.

The Y-rod is a forked stick made of hazel, apple or yew. That's the time-honored one used in many ancient pictures, and still used by traditional dowsers today, although some have moved on to ones made of plastic. The Y-rod brought about the term "water-witching" and indeed its historic use has been used for finding water. The two "handles" on the upper part of the Y-rod should have a firm tension or springiness.

The Y-rod is also useful for finding minerals such as oil, gold and various ores, plus archeological sites that may be hidden underground It can also find geopathic or negative energy zones which may be coming through your home, office or school. There is a section on negative energy zones coming up. Long-time dowser and author Sig Lonegrin has an excellent website showing how to use a Y-rod at www.geomancy.org. When you get there click on *"Dowsing"* and *"Y-rod."*

DOWSING LIKE A GUN-SLINGER

The L-rod looks like an L and the base forms the handle and the upright section of the L is the pointer. L-rods come in pairs and are very popular throughout the dowsing community. In the search position the two pointing arms are parallel, and when they reach the target they either become crossed or fly apart. They range in length from about five inches to 18 inches. The longer ones are more difficult to manipulate on windy days.

The American Society of Dowsers carries a variety of L-rods ranging from simple pieces of wire to ones with wooden and brass handles. Or you can make them yourself with a pair of wirecutters and pliers. Find two copper coat-hangers and cut two usable pieces, perhaps 18 or 20 inches in length. Bend a length of five inches for your handle, so that the wires form an L. Next lay your hands on two empty pen casings and slip them over the handles, then with the pliers, bend the bottom of the handles so the casings do not fall off. Because the arms may be sharp slip small electrical wire caps on the ends. The last thing you want is to be stabbed by your own dowsing rods.

USING THE L-RODS

There are two photos in this section showing the search position for the L-rods. The search position for using L-rods is to stand holding the handles in front of your chest with the arms pointing forward towards the horizon. Imagine you're holding two six-guns like an old time gunfighter. If there is a wind blowing, reduce the aim to just below the horizon, This is where shorter L-rods excel.

It is important in dowsing to focus on what you are searching for. Try not to let your mind get distracted. Concentrate on the object you wish to find.

Walk in the direction you are searching keeping your mind on your target. When you reach it, the L-rods will respond, either crossing or flying open. You can test your abilities on known underground objects, like water or gas lines coming through your property.

THE HARRY SANER EXERCISES

A real beginner's exercise was given by long-time dowser and energy specialist Harry Saner in the ASD's "American Dowser" (38/2). Harry crossed into Spirit earlier this year at the fine old age of 93. Mrs. Saner kindly gave me permission to use Harry's exercises in this book.

Go out into your backyard, pull out your garden hose, straighten it out, turn on the water, enough to get a small amount of water flowing and step back about 10 feet. Harry says with L-rods poised in the search position, walk forward slowly, concentrating on the water in that hose, but watch your rods, not the hose.

When you arrive over the hose those two L-rods might just cross each other. Look down and you will find that garden hose. "If the rods cross you are on your way to becoming a dowser," he said in the article..

Next, if you want to check which way water is flowing, hold one of the L-rods in your hand over the hose and ask "Show me which way the water is flowing." The arm of the L-rod will point in the direction the water is flowing. "Now you know you are a dowser," says Harry.

SEEKING HIDDEN OBJECTS

Once you get going and become confident in the use of L-rods and pendulums, you can scan vacation beaches for metal items that people may have lost like watches, rings, bracelets and more.

Once I saw a couple of youngsters armed with spades prodding the old railway right of way towards Cape Vincent. The tracks had long gone like the way of steam locomotives. The youngsters said they were looking for old metal spikes used to fasten the rails to the wooden ties. Pulling my L-rods from the back of the car, I walked with them for a few yards. They were amazed that in five minutes the rods showed several caches of spikes hidden a few inches underground.

L-rods are also excellent for finding "lost" objects in the home, but do not become disappointed if your first attempts fail. Remember, it's important to Practice! Practice! Practice!

What's all this got to do with Healing the Radical Spiritualist way? Read on, you may well be able to save someone's health, even his or her life by using your pendulum or your L-rods.

10

JAIME AND
THE DEADLY BEDROOM

T HE HEALING PATH of any Radical Spiritualist can become littered with stories that should not have happened. One involved a young mother. We will call her Jaime. She possessed a frail body under a mop of withering white hair.

At 33-years-of-age she had a studious youngster aged eight. She also had a husband, Steve, an accountant, who might have better used his bulky body as a bouncer at a nightclub. In his younger years he had been a military policeman, a perfect disciplinarian who toed an unbending line when it came to altered states and healing.

Jaime, battling cancer, was close to being treated with chemotherapy.

"You're a hypnotherapist," she said. *"I've heard that imagery can be a vital force in fighting cancer."* She declared her thoughts simply and factually in a calm voice. You did not have to be an intuitive to sense a desperate plea for help.

In the course of our initial consultation, she explained she had quit being a teacher to be an at-home mom, and to care for a sick mother. The family lived in a large tudor-style home perched on a plateau in the beautiful mountains of West Vancouver, British Columbia. Tears welled up in her eyes as she revealed her mother had died four years before.

"She had cancer too. We actually moved into her house so we could look after her. She bequeathed the house to us."

An alarm bell sounded in my head. I felt the presence of a spirit, no, two spirits! One was Chang my healing guide, the other was an entity appearing as a thin elderly man covered in ugly skin blemishes. He wore heavy framed spectacles and: *"I'm Harry. Tell her to move the bed. Please tell her."*

"Jaime, who was Harry?"

Jaime was startled. *"My dad. Why?"*

"He's here." Balding, horn-rimmed spectacles, wears two wedding rings.

Jaime smiled briefly. *"He married mum twice."*

"What's the problem with the bed?"

"Nothing," she shrugged. *"When mum died, we renovated the room and I sleep there. My husband sleeps at the other end of the house. We don't see eye to eye."* She shrugged helplessly. *"Why do you ask about the bed?"*

"Dad says he slept with your mother in that bed"

"Yes! That's right"

"And they both died of cancer, and now you have it too," I said gently. *"I would like to see your home, if I may."*

Within the hour we were standing in the garden of the tudor house perched on a rock plateau. Her bedroom window was above. I used my L-rods and found a band of negative energy coming through the rocks and passing right underneath her bedroom.

Upstairs in the room, the L-rods confirmed a strong geopathic zone of negative energy was running through the upper part of the bed, and anyone sleeping in the bed over a period of time, perhaps a year or two, would have a reduced immune system and suffer sickness. Dowsers have long called them *"cancer beds."*

"We can bounce the energy out of here by placing two breaker rods in the garden, one each on either side of the house.," I explained. *"That's the root core of your physical problem."*

We moved downstairs into the garden and I was taking two 30-inch copper rods from the trunk of my car, when a Jeep careened up the driveway. Steve, Jaime's husband arrived with a black thundercloud face. Steve pushed a protesting Jaime inside the house and reappeared a couple of minutes later.

"I told her I didn't want my wife seeing any wacky hypnotherapist. We are Christians and your sort of people work for the devil. So would you please get off our property, or I will call the police."

Steve did not realize it, but he was committing his wife to a death sentence. I reluctantly departed as requested. That afternoon, Jaime came for a series of discreet hypnosis sessions for imagery and later that week started her chemotherapy. She did ask what she could do about her bed. *"We do have a visitors room. I will sleep there."* My pendulum and Chang confirmed its safety.

Several months later, she came in with good news. *"My doctors say I'm clear. Thanks for your help in getting me out of that terrible bedroom,"* she said with a pleasant smile, then hesitated. *"Why was Steve so ada- mant about having you help us?"*

Shrugging, I told her that many men have serious blocks about any- thing their ego is not trained to hear. *"That's why there are more women leading the way in metaphysics, spiritual development and healing,"* I added.

"Just as a footnote, Steve's gone. He couldn't stand the stress of my be- ing sick," she said. *"So could you come over tomorrow and clear the house. I'd like to think that mum and dad's bedroom is quite safe. I'm sure they would like it that way."*

The shimmering image of the man with the horn-rimmed spectacles and the two wedding rings smiled behind Jaime. *"Your dad's giving you a thumbs up,"* I said.

She laughed happily. *"That's my dad. He did that whenever he was happy,"* she said, and then called out: *"Dad, thanks for letting us know. I love you. You know that. Tell Mum too."*

GEOPATHIC ZONES IN A NUTSHELL

So what did Jaime and her parents sleep on? What are geopathic zones?

Planet Earth revolves in a mass or energies. Ever since the nuclear aged dawned in 1945, most people have become aware of the existence of rays and radiation. Although invisible for the most part, they are acknowledged as infra red and ultra violet rays, microwaves, radio and television rays, radar, laser and cosmic rays and also solar rays.. At any one moment countless cell phone transmissions are zipping through your home and around your body. It's a fact of life.

But Planet Earth also radiates its own energy. It's positive, life-sustaining for the good of everything on the planet. But there are exceptions.

ENERGY GOES NEGATIVE

When earth energy encounters and transits through geological schists and fractures in rocks and strata formations, it changes from positive to negative. There is a 180 phase change. If you live in a mountain-area like our friend Jaime does, the phenomena occurs frequently. Volcanic rock formations are prone to create varieties of geopathic zones.

The earth is also laced with veins, much like the human body, but instead of blood these are veins of water, sometimes deep underground, sometimes just below the surface.

The veins, let's call them subterranean streams, vary in width and depth from a few inches to several feet. As the streams flow, the water may travel over clay, minerals and broken rock and again, the earth energy radiating through it changes polarity and becomes negative.

Subterranean running water will generate upward radiation and there is no rhyme nor reason for its routes, which may vary in any direction as a stream varies in direction on the surface. In other words, routes are as varied as surface streams. Straight lines rarely exist.

There is an interesting phenomena here. If a subterranean water vein at a depth of 100 feet below the earth's surface is twelve inches wide at its start, the beam of negative energy will be twelve inches wide when it comes to the surface, and it remains the same width at the top of a ten story highrise building.

Passing over such veins has little or no impact on the human body. But the trouble starts when a person regularly spends a lot of daily hours living, working or sleeping on a negative energy point. The places are known as Geopathic Zones. In Greek the word geo means earth and pathos stands for suffering.

116

The ancients who were more in tune with the earth than modern-day folk, "sensed" such places and avoided them. They read the signs. Even today you may notice that certain trees are disfigured either with bulges and warts, or split trunks and branches. Each tree is suffering and the malformations display this. If you find an area in your garden that fails to support good plant growth, check for a geopathic zone.

Even as I write this chapter at home in Chaumont, I was called out to help a family whose three-year old daughter was afraid of "something in the corner" of her bedroom. The family thought it was a negative spirit. When I arrived I told them: "There's no spirit, but a geopathic zone runs through her room." They asked how I knew: "The tree outside told me. It's grossly malformed and sits on the zone." My dowsing rods confirmed this.

Although the ancients avoided geopathic zones, the western hemisphere has received several wake-up calls. One in the 1920s when Gustav Freiherr Pohl who was working in Germany with a team of dowsers wrote "Earth Currents: Causative Factor of Cancer and Other Diseases." That stirred a number of people, but the major wake-up call came in the 1970s when Dr. Käthe Bachler's book "Earth Radiation" was published.

It showed alarming research on 11,000 cases in more than 3,000 places. It was clear, damning evidence that geopathic zones were causing harmful effects on those who lived on them. The zones reduced the effectiveness of the body's immune system and resulted in such illnesses as cancer, allergies, arthritis, insomnia, chronic fatigue, night-tremors, learning problems and many other afflictions. It told of family members systematically being killed because generation after generation was unconsciously sleeping on geopathic zones.

CANCER BEDS ROUTINELY KILLED

The Käthe Bachler study introduced the grim title of "cancer beds." It stunned medical fraternities in Germany and Austria. Doctors found that cures were only effective after exposure to noxious earth energies was eliminated. State and local governments took notice. The building of major projects such as schools and hospitals had to be free of geopathic zones.

Electronic sensor machines were developed but the dowser with his or her L-rods and pendulums was always the best method. In Europe today, many people when buying houses first have them checked for geopathic zones.

Because we did workshops and presentations on earth radiation around places in British Columbia and Washington State, wherever we went, we checked the places for radiation. For years I would check offices in which I worked. As I write this in my office study in Chaumont, upstate New York, a geopathic zone runs under my chair. Every few months I check the earth rods that are bouncing the energy over the house and protecting me.

The Käthe Bachler study showed how families, completely ignorant of what was happening in their home, saw one family member after another died in a "cancer bed." One person would die, so the family put another member in the bed, and when that person died of cancer, another unwittingly took their place. The study is filled with tragic stories.

SCHOOLS IN THE ZONE

Dr. Bachler also found that students studying in schools were affected. A student with a good study record, was innocently moved to a desk over a geopathic zone and is mentally affected. His studies and work become slack, and his memory and alertness are impacted. Older schools, built over geopathic zones subsequently started moving students around, and new schools were checked by dowsers prior to design and construction.

CURRY AND HARTMANN GRIDS

Earth energies are complicated with a number of earth energy grids, notably the Curry Grid discovered by Dr. Manfred Curry, MD and the Hartmann Grid.

Curry Grid lines were discovered by Dr. Curry in Germany. They run north-east to south-west and north-west to south-east. They form a network around the planet and occur every ten feet or so. Where two lines cross, the create an energy vortex. If the vortex coincides with a geopathic zone, it intensifies the effect, and makes the situation even more dangerous. If you are a dowser seeking this grid with L-rods or pendulums, you should focus on the "Curry Grid."

The Hartmann Grid named after another German medical practitioner runs north to south and east to west, and depending on the latitude range between six to twelve feet apart. They are known to vary and move according to time and place.

THE DOWSER HEALER AT WORK

Unless you are doing research or conducting special work, the dowser-healer does not need to to specify for what he/she is searching. And this includes water veins or cracks in the rock below ground. The key to healing a home, office or school is to ask your dowsing rods to show either "negative energy zones" or "zones of disturbance." The dowser should focus on this simple target.

INDICATORS OF ZONES IN THE BEDROOM

People spend up to a third of their lives in bed, six to nine hours a day on about twenty square feet. Therefore it is wise to be aware of symptoms and complaints that can arise through the presence of zones of disturbance. The dowser-healer will probably hear some of the following symptoms.

> *Refusal to go to bed. Opposition against going to bed.*
> *Insomnia. Unable to sleep for hours.*
> *Nightmares. Feelings of a "presence" in the bed or room.*
> *An aversion to certain spots in the bed.*
> *A feeling of "falling out of bed."*
> *Waking tired most mornings. Fatigue and apathy.*
> *Sleepwalking.*
> *Night sweats. Also feeling cold or shivering in bed.*
> *Nausea in the morning, even vomiting.*
> *Despondency, stress, depression.*

Frequent crying upon waking in the morning.
Rapid heart beat while lying still in bed. Cramps.
A person prefers sleeping on the couch instead of bed.

Naturally, only one of these symptoms is sufficient to indicate a problem. However, a person may experience several of these symptoms at one time.

INFANTS AND PRESCHOOLERS

Small babies, unable to move away, may react to a geopathic zone by showing signs of retarded development, prolonged crying, convulsive crying or screaming. We have experienced cases where babies have regularly crawled to a safe spot in their cribs simply to escape the zone of disturbance. Young children in beds, may take refuge from a geopathic zone by sleeping on the floor, or by wanting to sleep with others in the house.

CATS LOVE THE ZONES

A point to watch for: Cats love zones of disturbance and may well spend hours resting on a geopathic zone, even though it is slowly killing them. Ants and wild bees can always be found above the crossing of two subterranean currents. Hordes of gnats on a summer's evening will hover above zones of disturbance. Dogs detest the zones as do horses, cows, pigs, and birds.

Apple, pear and nut trees have an aversion to zones of disturbance as do currant bushes, lilacs and sunflowers. Indoors, begonias, azaleas and various cacti seek to avoid noxious rays.

Geopathic Zone seekers, these are plants seeking radiation from underground water currents. They include cherry, peach, plum, nectarine, elderberry, mistletoe and asparagus. Oak, fir and willow trees enjoy the negative radiation emanating from subterranean water flows. Malformed trees are usually standing on subterranean veins. Which is one good reason for not standing under such trees during a thunder and lightning storm. If you need to stand under any trees seek beech or linden because both are averse to negative earth energy.

SEEKING RELIEF

Once you have established where the geopathic zone runs in the house, and it affects beds, sofas and seats like computer places where someone spends considerable time, change the locations to safe areas. You can do this with a pendulum or L-rods as described earlier.

Here's a useful oddity: If you cannot move the bed because of space restrictions and there is no other room available, first remove the mattress. Next on the boxspring place a one layer of plastic – large garbage bags do well. It should cover the sleeping area. Then replace the mattress on the bed. Plastic is an energy blocker and it will block the negative energy coming through for about three months. After that the effectiveness starts to deteriorate and it needs to be changed.

If the exposure of a person has existed for a short time, you can expect a complete recovery in a few days. Depending on the length of exposure, and the physical condition of the person, recovery may take longer. If an illness is in an advanced stage, there may be no noticeable improvement at all, but move the person anyway. If there is any chance of improvement, it will come from being in a safe place.

SOME SICK PEOPLE BECOME ATTACHED

There are some oddities in all of this that bend the mind. For instance, if Aunt Mary is chronically sick and has been sleeping on a geopathic zone for several years, well-meaning family may meet strong objections when trying to move Mary's bed.

Crazy as it sounds, Aunt Mary has become unconsciously attached to the zone and demands the bed be pushed back to its original position. The way out of this is to move the bed a couple of inches every day until it is completely clear.

Another oddity: Someone who has been living on a geopathic zone in an apartment, feels that a new home would offer a better life. When looking for a new place they will roam through it and the moment they unknowingly walk across a geopathic zone they may well declare "This is the place. I'll take it." The bed will be placed exactly on the zone.

BOUNCING ENERGY OVER YOUR HOME

As a dowser you can bounce the geopathic zone's effects right over your house, creating a safety zone underneath. Or you may offer your services to clear a friend's place. Here's what you need to clear a building.

Two L-rods, a pendulum, a few stakes or wooden markers and several copper or steel welding rods. They should be about one-eighth of an inch thick and about 30 inches long. The welding rods can be obtained at your local welding supply store. A large hammer is useful.

When you are first checking out a house, wander round and see if there are any malformed trees. This could be your first indicator. Access the house and walk from room to room to see where geopathic zones run.

Next, make a complete circle slowly walking round the outside of the building using the L-rods parallel and pointing to the horizon. As you walk focus and ask the L-rods to *"Show me any negative zones."*

When you come to a zone, place a marker such as a stake or even a rock on the spot and continue searching. Normally you will find one going into the house, and one coming out. Find the second one and mark it.

THE MYSTERIOUS NUMBERS

Now, keep in mind that when you bounce earth energy up over a house, it angles up at 63 degrees and comes down at 63 degrees. Why, no one seems to know. It's a mystery. Six and three form a nine number and a nine is the mystery number of the Universe.

When you place the zone breakers, the copper/steel rods in the ground on either side of the house, you have to judge that the angle is right, particularly if there are bedrooms upstairs. The negative energy has to clear the house or building so you may have to follow the zone away from the house to ensure the rays will bounce over the place.

Using your pendulum check the depth of the water vein, its width and flow. You do this using the elimination technique described earler. Hold one of the L-rods over the water vein and ask it to show you which direction the water is running. It will swing in that direction. (Remember the hose exercise earlier?)

Tracing the geopathic zone away from the house, find a position that will clear the house. Then bury a welding rod so that it lies across the zone. Then go round the other side of the house and do the same to that part of the zone. Burying keeps people accidentally moving rods which is why som dowsers carry a hammer or even a small spade.

Then check the inside of the house to see that it is clear of the noxious rays.

BOOKS AND SOURCES

The process I have explained is quite basic, but it will get you to safeguard your home or help a neighbor. There is much more to learn on dowsing in general and geopathic zones in particular. The best way is, as my old buddy Tom Passey would say: "Practice! Practice! Practice!" By practicing you make mistakes and that's a fast track to learning how to succeed.

It is worth while joining a dowsers' society or chapter, or attending workshops or classes. The American Society of Dowsers has much information on their website at www.dowsers.org and the Candian Society of Questers in Western Canada can be found at www.questers.ca and The Canadian Society of Dowsers in Eastern Canada is at http://canadiandowsers.org. There are several reference works listed at the end of this book.

One word of parting advice on this healing subject, if you're a beginner and have questions, talk to a local dowser. They are normally extremely approachable, or you can go online to any of the associations mentioned above and email them asking for dowsers in your area.

As you tread this healing path, you will quickly realize that through dowsing you have the ability to save lives. Accept the fact with a little smile and thank the Universe or whoever you pray to for giving you the privilege.

11

PRANA,
MORE THAN JUST ENERGY

O NE OF THE ACUTE DOWNSIDES of being a journalist, news photographer, broadcaster and editor is that the stress and excitement inherent in the profession drives one to do strange things, like smoking. In my twenty-five year stint in reporting , I was smoking between twenty and forty cigarettes a day.

One day in Kamloops, British Columbia while walking up the stairs to CHNL Radio I sensed that my breathing was becoming shallow and strained. Those were the days before metaphysics, mysticism and logical thinking had dawned in my life. Standing at the top of the stairs, I looked back down the steps and a woman's voice echoed upwards: "Better that you stop smoking, Bobbie. Now!"

Thinking it was my imagination, I made a decision to quit—but not now. There were stories to do, assignments to complete. But I did cut back to twenty cigarettes a day. Quitting a major habit that had been part of my life for a quarter of a century was not easy. I put it on the back shelf.

A year later I found myself in another high pressure job, manager of public relations for Weyerhauser Canada, looking after operations in British Columbia, Ontario and Quebec.

Chairman Tom Rust was enthusiastic about an audio-slide show I had created called *From the Woods to the World.* So much so, he wanted to show employees and families across Canada. Two weeks later with lots of coffees and smokes in my body, I reached home, hoping to relax. I had supper with Lucy and the children. And then, it happened.

As usual after supper, I had reached for a cigarette, lit it and took a breath. It wasn't there! Horrified, I felt as if I couldn't breath. A heavy weight straddled my chest. Thoughts of suffocation flooded my mind. Heart attack? This can't be happening. Not to me. I'm only in my early forties. Not saying anything, I ran to the outside door and stood on the steps. The cigarette flicked off into the garden.

Still trying to breath normally, my body feeling strangely odd, my mind totally bewildered, I decided to walk by the cool, relaxing trees flanking the North Thompson River. Perhaps it was not a heart attack. What was it? I walked for maybe half an hour, and slowly my breathing came back to normal. It was still shallow, but at least it felt better than before.

Completely shaken, I resolved never to smoke again, and to back it up, I resolved to ditch coffee too. The tightness in my chest slipped away. The following days and weeks were tough as the ghost of smoking haunted me, but I had experienced a severe lesson I would never forget. Smoking? Never again.

SO I WAS FOOLED

Two years later in Vancouver, I was now media relations manager for the Insurance Corporation where we had regular physical examinations. The doctor wanted to know if I had had any problem breathing because, he said, "You have a hiatal hernia."

"Hiatal hernia is the protrusion of the upper part of the stomach into the thorax through a tear or weakness in the diaphragm," he explained. "It's a fairly common condition that can be inflamed by irritants such as smoking and coffee, otherwise you're in good health. Work to get some of the weight off. You might want to look at the Yogi Complete Breath. Your breathing is a bit shallow. "

Later that day I came to the realization that I had been fooled into thinking I was having a heart attack. Whoever was out there, up there,

God whatever, I sent thanks. I realized I had no desire for a cigarette which was wonderful.

THE OPPORTUNITY FOR OPTIMAL HEALTH

That night I started nightly walks which eventually evolved into jogging along the seawall at English Bay. I also heard about meditation, metaphysics and higher awareness, and started reading books. Among them was one called "The Hindu-Yogi Science of Breath," by Yogi Ramacharaka.

On page 39 I discovered "How to acquire the Yogi Complete Breath," and for those interested in healthy bodies, it's a valuable gem, if you are passionate about maintaining optimum health, it is all there in 88 pages. I discovered there is more, much more to breathing than just taking in air into the body. It's a major spiritual function.

According to Ramacharaka, Yogis classify Respiration into four general methods. (1)High Breathing; (2) Mid Breathing; (3) Low Breathing; and (4) Yogi Complete Breathing.

High Breathing in the upper part of the chest and lungs is the smallest section of the Respiratory system and uses a minimum amount of air. Yogis say it is probably the worst form of breathing known to humanity, and requires a lot of energy for a small benefit. Typically it is wasting energy with poor returns. It is common among Western races, simply because full breathing is not taught in general upbringing and education. High Breathingis also known as "mouth breathing."

Mid Breathing or Rib Breathing as it is known is not much better. This is where the diaphragm is pushed upward and the abdomen is drawn in. It's a common practice among people who think they are breathing deeply.

Low Breathing has been exploited by Western trainers as "Abdominal Breathing" and "Diaphragmic Breathing." It has helped many people to overcome traditional respiratory afflictions.

The Yogi Complete Breath brings not only health and healing benefits, but esoteric and spiritual benefits as well. Before we examine the Complete Breath, let us explore the mystical esoteric theory of breath.

PRANA, THE VITAL FORCE

I once saw an advertisement in one of the supermarket tabloids for "Pranic Therapy Ointment." A client bought it. It resembled and smelled like petroleum jelly and reeked of "scam." I do not think the makers had any idea of what Prana really is.

The teachers in all ages and lands have normally taught the secret of Prana in the mystery schools, in spiritual development groups and to those genuinely interested. The secret? Oriental Yogis taught that there is to be found in the air a substance or principle from which all life is derived.Prana comes from the ancient Sanscrit term meaning "Absolute Energy" or "Vital Force." It can be found in all forms of life from the smallest amoeba to human beings. It extends through all plant life to the highest form of animal life. As the Yogis say, Prana is all pervading.

Every cell in your body, every atom, every molecule, even your DNA is motivated by Prana, the energy force, the vital force that drives all life.

It is difficult to pinpoint. It is similar to light, only more abstract. With light you can only see it either at its origin, such as emanating from the sun or a star, or a light bulb or a candle flame, and then when it is reflected off something. You cannot with human eyes see light while it's travelling. The problem with Prana is you cannot see the source, but it floods the Universe.

Prana is in the air, but it is far from being air. It contains no chemical constituents but it motivates chemicals. It travels with air, but does not need air to move. It can be found in space, but it will be dormant unless it encounters a physical structure that it can affect. All living creatures need Prana to live, but it exists as a virtually independent energy force. Scientists ignore it simply because they have no visible measuring instrument, but I am sure that somewhere out there, there is a boffin working to create a practical measuring instrument.

THE VITAL BREATH OF THE SPIRIT

Whoever penned the book of Genesis recognized the difference between atmospheric air and the "mysterious and potent principle" contained within it. Yogi Ramacharaka, author of "Science of Breath" comments on this by writing: *"He speaks of neshmet ruach chayim, which translated means "the breath of the spirit of life."*

This breath of the Spirit is life energy, also known as chi, ki and prana. It is the vital force that runs through the body, mind and soul and constitutes the Life Force. This Spirit of Life is the energy that mysteriously heals the human body after an accident or a surgical operation. Medical practitioners do not heal, neither do the great variety of healers. Each practitioner sets the condition for Prana to heal.

THE POWER OF THE FORCE

The Sufi Master Hazrat Inayat Kahn who was a great musician and brought the ancient Sufi teachings to the West in the first part of the twentieth century, wrote: *"The healing power of Christ, the magnetism of Mohammed, the miraculous power of Moses, the charm of Krishna, and the inspiration of the Buddha, all these were attained by breath."* According to the *Neijing Suwen: The Yellow Emperor's Classic Book of Internal Chinese Medicine,* the universe is composed of various forces and principles, such as Yin and Yang, Qi and the Five Elements (or phases). These forces can be understood via rational means and people can stay in balance or return to balance and health by understanding the laws of these natural forces.

The *Neijing Suwen* also indicates that Prana, the Vital Force can aid in longevity. *"In ancient times, there were the so-called spiritual men; they mastered the universe, and controlled yin and yang. They breathed the essence of life and were independent in preserving the spirit. Their muscles and flesh remained unchanged."*

Is this why some of the early Biblical characters lived so long? Adam 930 years; Noah 950; Moses 120; Abraham 175? One has to question the validity of these ages. Other religious leaders did not live so long. Buddha was about 80 when he crossed over, Lao Tzu was 69; Confucius 72 and Muhammed 63. Zoroaster is out of the running because he is said to have been murdered at age 77 by so-called infidels, while he was praying at an altar.

SWIMMING THE RIVER OF LIFE

There is little doubt that Prana, the breath of the spirit of life, if it is respected as the Vital Force will carry a person through a charmed life. It's much like trying to swim directly across a fast flowing river. One is likely to be overwhelmed, but if you swim with the current, the Vital Force, you will reach the far shore safely and reap substantial benefits.

Prana will not only strengthen all parts of the human body, mind and spirit, it will also allow itself to be accumulated and reserved. This is important if one is developing metaphysical faculties such as mediumship, psychic gifts and healing. You can feel and benefit from the flow of Prana into your body by going back to Chapter Three and performing *The Healing Tree* exercise.

As Ramacharaka writes: *"One who has mastered the science of storing away Prana, either consciously or unconsciously, often radiates vitality and strength which is felt by those coming in contact with him, and such a person may impart this strength to others, and give them increased vitality and strength."*

This is the basis of a number of healing modalities, hand-on healing, Therapeutic Touch, magnetic healing, Reiki and the Spiritualists' Spirit Healing, although many of the practitioners are not aware of what the power is.

Many Spiritualist healers believe the healing power comes from spirits in the upper regions. Actually, the Vital Force, the Prana exists in all areas of the Universe. When a Spiritualist healer works with a healee, a patient, and is assisted by a healing guide, the actual guide is simply channeling Prana from the Universe, or better still, the Universal Mind, Infinite Intelligence.

If a healer were to use his or her own reserves of Prana, they would find the energy might suffice for one or two people, but after that, the reserves would quickly be depleted and the would-be healer would feel weak and perhaps dizzy.

It is of the utmost importance that a healer (1) should maintain a healthy lifestyle that includes complete breathing, and (2) acknowledge and attunes to the Universal Reservoirs of Prana, the Vital Force.

LIVING WITH THE COMPLETE BREATH

As you may have gathered by now, the Complete Breath brings a bounty of benefits. For starters it's a great way for recharging mind and body energy. It calms the nervous system, reduces stress and in fact it has been known to lift depression. In addition it brings increased oxygen to your body, purifies the bloodstream and enriches it. With more oxygen flowing through the system, your skin starts to look better, even younger. Yes, oxygen is an important food.

The Complete Breath, if maintained daily, will realize development of the chest and the diaphragm and it empowers the lungs to work better. It strengthens the thorax, that cavity known as the chest which houses your heart, lungs, and esophagus. It also improves the abdomen. Long term benefits include a growing resistance to colds and improved digestion.

Performing the Complete Breath on a regular basis is of great assistance to people who rely on breathing, particularly in sports activities such as swimming and running. In addition, musicians who perform on wind instruments, bugles, trumpets and particularly the Australian didgeridoo benefit greatly from the Complete Breath.

If you have recently stopped smoking and your lungs are functioning reasonably well, the Complete Breath invigorates your body, reduces withdrawal stress, and starts to rehabilitate your inner system. Check with your health professional to see if this activity is right for you.

If you are a practicing healer or simply wish to heal yourself and benefit from feeling the Vital Force flowing through your body, mind and spirit, here's what to do.

EXERCISE: THE BREATH OF LIFE

1. Stand or sit comfortably in a straight-backed chair. Close your eyes.
2. Make sure your back is comfortably straight. This will straighten your chest (thorax) for easier breathing.
3. Breathe in slowly and deeply through your nose.

4. Make sure the air is going to the lower part of your lungs. Allow the rib cage to expand and push out on the abdomen.
5. Then concentrate on filling the upper part of your lungs and feel your chest expanding. The abdomen will tighten up slightly.
6. Hold the breath for a few seconds, perhaps five if you can.
7. Then holding your chest up, in the expanded position, exhale slowly, pulling the abdomen in as you breathe out. Keep your chest puffed up, if possible.
8. Repeat five to seven times.

Once you can perform the Complete Breath with confidence, it helps to establish a rhythm, particularly with pushing the abdomen out as you breathe in and pulling the abdomen in as you breathe out. It helps if you can do an extra snort as you finish breathing out. This helps to clear the bottom of your lungs of stale air.

REVITALIZING MIND AND BODY

If you are performing this properly, you will find yourself wanting to do it every day. It quickly revitalizes both your mind and body and eliminates end-of-day fatigue and improves digestion and reduces common breathing problems. After a few days, you will probably wonder why you had not done this earlier in your life. It never ceases to amaze me why the Complete Breath is not taught to students in schools and people in churches.

Once you accomplish the Complete Breath, you may well find yourself taking time out to do it several times a day, and if you can allow deep breathing to become a part of your life, you will sense all-round benefits coming into your being. You may not live as long as the ancients did, but you will certainly stand a good chance of living a longer, healthier life. And you'll probably look a lot better too.

GETTING OUT OF THE "RUT"

It's a sad fact of life, most people are programmed to get old simply through thoughts and conditioning.

"You'll have to retire at sixty-five, then what are you going to do?"
"Aunt Nelly died last year at sixty. Everyone said she would. It's in the
genes, you know." "Cancer runs in our family. Takes everyone before they
can really get old." "Grandma lived to ninety-five. She spent half her life
being old." "You're too old to go hiking?"

I like to think of such damaging remarks as mental and spiritual terrorism. Here's why.

Our lives are full of suggestions and because some strike an emotional cords, the subconscious mind absorbs and merges them with a whole
lot of other similar suggestions. Suggestive thoughts result from watching
television, participating in social groups on the internet, or from reading
newspapers and magazines, or somebody in our personal environment
told us.

Remember the Self-Talk Suggestions earlier in this book? Well,
there's a whole bunch of folk out there, known as advertising moguls,
who attempt, and quite often succeed in programming millions of people
with a galaxy of negative possibilities. If you fail to hear or note them
consciously, your marvelous subconscious mind faithfully records and
stores them in your memory banks. It happens. The moguls spend
billions of dollars creating buying patterns in the human mind.

For instance, how many times do you hear the TV ad instructing you
to "Talk to your doctor." It happens several times an hour, particularly
during national news broadcasts at supper time.

A drug for controlling blood sugar in type-2 diabetics. There's no
problem with that. The real problem comes when a television viewer
consciously or subconsciously hears such words as *"Health effects*
associated with this drug use include an increased risk for heart attack,
congestive heart failure, vision loss, and liver failure." The advertisement
is repeated several times during the hour and the information starts
accumulating in the subconscious mind.

A person using the drug is already under stress and starts thinking –
my vision is not so good, maybe I'm getting some of those other things,
like liver failure...or maybe a heart attack." They test their pulse. It seems
fast. They remember the words "Ask your doctor." Next morning they are

seated waiting to see their physician. People have been programmed through repeated suggestions to *"Talk to your doctor."* And we wonder why the American Health System is so bogged down.

The more people hear or see warning words on television or in the print media, the more they visualize it happening. As we explained at the beginning of this book, whatever you imagine in your body actually happens. If you imagine you're relaxed you will be relaxed, if you imagine you're well, you will be well, if you imagine you're sick...

The question now is: Are Americans being systematically programmed to be sick?

MEMO TO SPIRITUAL GROUPS: Start a nondenominational "Relax and Let Go" weekly circle. Nine out of ten people feel stressed - and suffer physical illnesses because of it. Objective: Reducing stress improves your life. Reflect on daily stressors, demonstrate relaxation and meditation, teach breathing, positive imagery, exercise and encourage good eating. Bring in special guest speakers.

BEAT THE "GETTING OLD"PROGRAMMING

Society likes us to grow old. It confuses the system if you do not conform. Never tell your life insurance agent that you plan to stay healthy and live to ninety, they may go into shock.

When you live in the Here and Now, the Prana, the Vital Force in your body starts to vibrate on a higher loving rate. Your body is not feeling the burden of negative past memories or concerns for the future. You are living in the Now.

Here are some practices you can do to stay healthy and feel young. Each one of these suggestions is like a meditation, a time to be with yourself, a special time. It does not have to be long, perhaps a few minutes ranging from ten to thirty minutes, whatever feels good for you. And they will pull you into the Here and Now.

LISTEN TO THE RAIN: On a rainy day, sit on the porch and watch and listen to the rain on the window or roof. Be totally with the rain as it washes and cleans everything that you can see. If you enjoy walking in the rain do that, perhaps carry an umbrella. Be with the rain in the Now.

The sound and feeling of the rain is washing away any stress, any tension, any negative thoughts. Sense your body relaxing and letting go. How does it feel listening to the rain? If old memories surface, observe them without judgment or comment and let them go where they will.

A FINE DAY WITH PRANA: Walking on a fine day is excellent for recharging body and mind energies with Prana. If you are in the open country, try this for energy building. Stand facing the sun, but don't look at it. Feet spaced comfortably apart, hands and arms in the upside down Y shape. Close your eyes and perform the Yogi Complete Breath, slowly and easily. Do it ten times. When complete, thank whoever you pray to and walk home. As you do, you may well notice your hands tingling. That is Prana, and if you have someone sick at home, you may ask if you can lay your hands on their shoulders for a few minutes. They will probably enjoy it.

THE BAREFOOT MEDITATOR: Here is something I always enjoy. Walking barefoot on a clean, hard road or paved sidewalk for a few minutes. Walk slowly and watch your feet. Be in the Here and Now and be conscious of your body as your feet connect with the earth. Know that you are part of the Planet which in turn is part of the Solar System and the Universe. When you finish walking, sit on a bench , close your eyes and feel centered. This is excellent for grounding.

SENSING THE NATURAL WORLD: Find a quiet place such as a good cave, a seaside cove or a clearing in the forest. Be in the Here and Now. Totally impartial. Sit still and listen to your body. Observe it steadily relaxing. You may well hear your pulse, your heart beats slowing down. Sense any discomforts and stressors, dissolving from your body. Next, listen to the world around you. What are the sounds? Where do they originate? What are they saying? Sense the energy around you. Can you hear the trees breathing? Be patient. Do not strain to listen. Simply let the sounds and the feelings come. You will be pleasantly surprised at how your super-senses are developing.

KIDS STUFF FOR ADULTS

The following exercises are fun things for adults to do. If you hesitate and start to make excuses, impartially observe your thoughts, your hesitations. Are there limitations holding you back? If so, where did you find them? Is your False Self blocking you? Observe these things without comment, judgment or opinion. If your partner says *"You're too old for that sort of thing,"* stay cool and ask them to join you.

SWINGING ON A GATE: If you can find one of those sturdy wooden gates like they have on farms, get on and swing on it like you did when you were a young. You will be surprised at your reaction. Allow yourself to express your feelings. Cheer, smile, shout, scream, sing, or laugh. Finally, when you've had enough, find a seat somewhere, center your consciousness and check how your body, mind and spirit feel.

A WALK ON THE BEACH: There are other possibilities for feeling and sensing the Earth and Nature. Consider going to the beach and skipping pebbles on the water; walk in soft wet sand after the tide has gone out, and watch your feet sink into it. Allow your feet and body to sense the power of the sand, Mother Earth. Feel the closeness of yourself and the Universe. Finish your time on the beach by walking through every tide-pool you can see. If you find some beautiful shells, wash them off and take them home. Find a place to put them as a reminder of your time on the beach.

THE OLD AMERICAN ROPE TRICK: I dislike saying this, but you might check with some health professional before doing this next *"fun thing."* Get a rope and practice skipping in your yard or garden. Then when you feel competent, go skipping along your neighborhood sidewalk. If you get some comments from neighbors, ask them to join you. Start a block skipping group. As usual, when you have finished, find a place, probably at home, to meditate on your feelings.

MAKING DAISY CHAINS: Something for a summer's day: find a meadow, a paddock or even a park and sit down on the grass and make daisy chains. How to make one? Pick a number of daisies – twenty should do. Make sure they have longish stalks.

Take a stalk and make a little slice in it with a finger nail, then take the next daisy and slot its stalk through the slice on the first daisy stalk. Keep on repeating. And lo! You have a daisy chain! Ask the daisies if it is all right to do this. This activity along with gardening, really puts you back in touch with Mother Earth and the planet.

A LAZY DAY WATCHING CLOUDS: While you are in a meadow, or even in a good park, or even a lawn at home, on a sunny day relax on the grass and simply watch the clouds drifting lazily on their way.

Observe how the clouds continually change form, and as you watch some will appear out of nowhere and others will disappear. Pick a small cloud and imagine, just imagine, you can make it disappear, and see what happens. Then watch anything in the sky that comes into view. A bird or even an aircraft. Observe your thoughts as you watch. If there is a large expanse of blue sky, observe it. Feel the space. Sense the power of the Universe. As you do this, realize that you have nothing to do, nowhere to go, nothing to think about, just feel you are part of the Cosmos. Do this for at least ten minutes, perhaps half an hour, and then be conscious of any changes in your body, mind and spirit.

MAKING FACES: As your age progresses you may well notice that your face adopts heavy lines. Creases. The skin loses its flexibility. No matter what age you are, perform this on a regular basis, like every day. While carrying out your toilets in the morning, washing, showering, shaving, ready for make-up, gaze at your face in the mirror. Remember the teachings: no judging, no comments, no opinions, just live in the Here and Now.

When you feel ready, start making faces at yourself. Change your face to express the following words and hold the "face" for at least five to ten seconds or a slow count of one to ten.

Small smile, happy smile, broad grin, stupid grin, frown, angry frown, bright smile, gloomy, sad, very sad, frightened, aloof, laughing, ear-to-ear grin, small smile, relax.

These should take two to three minutes. Note how your face feels afterwards. You may well feel sensations from muscles you did not know they were there.

After performing this exercise on a daily basis for a few weeks you will notice that the skin on your face becomes more supple and alive, and overall, you will start to feel better and more alive.

How many people exercise their face muscles? We go to the YMCA three mornings a week and I rarely, if ever, see anyone exercising their faces. The face is the most important and single identification feature in peoples' lives yet it's the feature most ignored when it comes to exercising and natural revitalization.

If you cannot perform the above exercise, do this one. Make a broad grin at yourself in the mirror, and hold it there for thirty seconds. Look at yourself. Look into your eyes. Your energy will change.

FUN THINGS TO DO IN SUMMARY

Pick one or two of the activities and do them on a regular basis, and after a few weeks observe how you feel. You may well find your energy building up and changing positively. Other benefits will occur, such as gaining fresh confidence in life.

Just don't play golf, like millions of others do to ease the boredom of retirement, home or office work. If you like golf, put on a baseball cap backwards and become a golf caddy. Volunteer. The worst they can do is pay you. It will give you exercise, you'll hear lots of gossip, possibly hear some investment tips and your lungs will enjoy the fresh air. And you will avoid the stress of winning at golf.

Chances are some of these activities will make you react and declare: *"I feel foolish," "I can't possibly do that,"* or *"I feel really childish."*

Childish? If you do, that's what it's all about. It's learning to be a kid again and there's no law against it, in fact the Universe is with you. The Universal Law of Attraction will bring other similar minded folk into your life.

However, if you do have some serious blocks in performing the exercises I mentioned earlier – remember Impartial Self Observation, and do it without judgment, opinion, comment etc., and see what happens. You will be glad you did.

REMEMBER TO LAUGH!

One more thing. In the foregoing exercises it is likely that you laughed and felt the energy move through your body.

Someone once said that *"Laughter is the best medicine,"* and this has been proved many times. Lord Byron said of laughter: *"It is cheap medicine."* And so it is.

In a world where stress levels are soaring faster than a moon rocket and the rigors of the daily grind are getting you down, you would be surprised at what laughter can do for you.

Various researchers have shown that laughing lowers blood pressure, reduces stress, triggers the release of endorphins-- the body's natural painkillers--and produces a general sense of well-being. It is the key to a happier and much more healthier life.

Have you ever heard of Laughter Yoga? It is the brainchild of Dr.Madan Kataria, a physician from Mumbai, India who, with just a small group of people, launched the first Laughter Club in 1995. Today, Laughter Yoga has more than 6,000 Social Laughter Clubs in about 60 countries.

How does it work? It combines unconditional laughter with Yogic Breathing (Pranayama). Anyone can laugh for no reason, without relying on humor, jokes or comedy. Laughter is simulated as a body exercise in a group; with eye contact and childlike playfulness and it soon turns into real and contagious laughter.

The concept is based on a scientific fact that the body cannot differentiate between fake and real laughter. Real or false laughter gets the same physiological and psychological benefits. You will find them at www.laughteryoga.org.

A MEDITATION IN SMILING

Laughter is invigorating and so is smiling. The old Taoist teachers said that both laughter and smiling created good health, happiness and a longer life.

In your favorite place for meditation and relaxation, bring a soft smile to your face and close your eyes. Continue to smile as you focus on your breathing. If you wish to go to your Sanctuary of the Mind and do the rest of the exercise there, that's fine. You can do this anywhere that's quiet.

Feel the smile on your face. You will sense the energy already spreading to different parts of your head. Say: *"I fill my head with smiles and laughter."*

Next focus on your neck and shoulders and say: *"I fill my neck and my shoulders with smiles and laughter."* Work slowly through your entire body, addressing each part as you did the first. Address each part: hands, arms, chest, heart, back, waist, stomach, internal organs, thighs, legs, ankles and feet. You may also include such parts as your bowels and private parts.

When you have finished, conclude by saying: *"I fill my entire body with smiles and laughter. I send love and appreciation to every cell in my body."*

Spend several minutes relaxing within. Sense any new energies moving around your body. Then rise and get on with your life.

Throughout the meditation it is good if you can sustain a physical smile on your face, but do not worry if you fail, your body will understand and love you for it anyway.

12

JERICHO AND
THE POWER OF SOUND

ISN'T IT INTRIGUING that when someone mentions a particular word, the human memory, the subconscious mind immediately responds in less than a second. With me it happens when someone says *"Jericho."*

The community of Jericho is a hop skip and a jump north of the Dead Sea in Jordan. It's midway between Amman and Jerusalem. Most people will associate Jericho with that walled fortress in the Old Testament dramatically featured in the Book of Joshua.

Joshua was one of the twelve spies Moses sent to explore the land of Canaan. After Moses crossed into Spirit, Joshua led the tribes of Israel and it was at Jericho that the Bible says God gave Joshua the following instructions.

"And ye shall compass the city, all you men of war, and go round about the city once. Thus shalt thou do for six days. Seven priests shall bear before the Ark of the Covenant seven trumpets of rams' horns: and the seventh day ye shall compass the city seven times, and the priests shall blow with the trumpets. And it shall come to pass, that when they make a long blast with the ram's horn, and when ye hear the sound of the trumpets all the people shall shout with a great shout; and the wall of the city shall fall down flat." (Bible: Joshua 6)

The power of sound! Can you imagine the walls of the great fortress tumbling down? When I was a kid in school, a teacher named Mr. Clough (pronounced Cluff) used to talk about it, because he appreciated history and the power of sound. I recall his voice: *"You can heal with sound and you can destroy with sound."* I failed to understand those words then , but I never forgot them.

Years later, I still didn't understand even when as a reporter living in Jordan, the United Press editor in London phoned: *"Get over to Jericho and interview archeologist Dr. Kathleen Kenyon."* Then he added: *"You'd better read Joshua Six before you head out. And ask her about the walls."*

Tubby Abrahams, a veteran news photographer at Keystone who had been in the Spanish Civil War started me on news photography. He always advised: *"Shoot on the way in. It's insurance."* Words of wisdom!

As I arrived at the archeological dig the work area covered a large dusty mound, the size of a soccer field. The way in was through an encampment of faded white tents, tables, and canvas sheets on the sand covered with countless artifacts that included chunks of human bones including skulls. My two Rolleiflexes recorded the scene..

In the center of the field was a neatly carved but gaping hole in which you could easily drop a a couple of transit buses. Terraces and ladders lined the walls and a small army of Arabs feverishly worked different levels.

Wham! She came out of nowhere. A feisty English woman with eyes peering pointedly from under a large dusty hat. The eyes wanted to tear me apart. Not given to trite conversation, she was a woman of few words. Once you had met her, she had a place in your memory banks forever.

"Journalist, eh? Well, there's nothing to see and I have nothing to say. Archeologists make their living from writing papers for publication, you know."

Attempting to ignore my non-welcome, I asked her about Joshua, the trumpets and the walls of Jericho tumbling down.

"Never happened," she said bluntly. *"The walls came down before Joshua arrived. Probably from an earthquake. Interesting story but it probably never happened."* She smiled politely. *"Excuse me. Must go. Work, you know."*

142

At a coffeeshop in modern Jericho, a mile or so from the Kenyon dig, my taxi driver and the shop owner named Asa filled me in.

They told me that Dr. Kenyon was the daughter of a director of the British Museum. She had spent seven years in the Holy Land excavating Tel es-Sultan – the world's oldest civilized city.

They said 11,000 years ago there were Neolithic inhabitants living in pit dwellings. They had domesticated animals and produced decorated pottery. *"During the Bronze Age the need to defend the settlement led to the construction of massive city walls and towers,"* said the coffeeshop owner. Asa brought out a shard of pottery which he claimed came from the dig. *"You want to buy?"* he asked, expectantly?

"No, thanks," I said, but an American woman from Ohio, who had overheard our conversation, glady accepted and gave Asa two hundred American dollars.

When the woman had gone, I asked the coffeeshop owner if he believed the Joshua story and the Bible story that the walls came tumbling down through the use of sound.

"Of course," nodded the man. *"It's good for business."* The two men both laughed. Asa brought out another shard of pottery and said: *"I give you for fifty dinar."*

I never ceased to be amazed at what information one could obtain in an Arab coffee shop in Jericho. It was 1958. I still did not know how sound worked, but years later I was to find out that the Joshua report might well have happened.

RIPPLES IN THE SAND

Fast forward to 2006. My partner, Betty Lou and I are studying the power of sound and the story of Dr. Hans Jenny, the Swiss scientist who discovered an interesting phenomenon and named it Cymatics, the study of wave phenomena.

Jenny placed a layer of sand on a metal plate. Underneath he placed an oscillator or vibrator and switched it on

The grains of sand were immediately tormented in a chaos and bounced up and down. Then, something amazing occurred. They formed an intricate and amazing pattern.

Dr. Jenny changed the oscillator frequency. The sand responded and bloomed into another fascinating pattern. Subsequent experiments showed that sound vibrations produce images in not only sand, but water, clay and other mediums. Sound has the power of creation. Low tones produce simple and clear pictures, while higher tones create more complex patterns..

Dr Jenny invented a device called a tonoscope, which used a membrane stretched over a frame, much like a drum. It was at this point he discovered the human voice could also create patterns in the sand. And it was all done without electronics, simply the power of the human voice .

For 14 years Jenny conducted sound effects animating sands, powders, liquids, creating flowing forms that mirrored designs and patterns found in nature. His two volume work "Cymatics: A Study in Wave Phenomena" is invaluable for students of metaphysics, sound healing, sacred geometry, and something the Hindus call Nada Brahma, the audible life stream which we will discuss later.

THE ANCIENT ART OF SACRED SOUNDS

We are living in extraordinary times—times of enormous shifts in awareness, and times of great changes in cultures and societies. It is also a time of great change in world consciousness.

The keys of this consciousness have been known since the dawn of people, the dawn of spiritual beings. At the beginning of this book, we saw ancient folk drawing and painting images and making sounds they knew would attract the goddess, a spirit from the higher levels. They were the first mediums, the first spirit communicators. The first spiritualists.

The ancients knew the power of sound, including the scribe who penned the Book of Joshua. They called it Sacred Sound because it was special, it was magical. The technique is written in the Upanishads, the sacred book of Hinduism that "sound is your essence."

144

Shabd is their name for sound, the great sound, the audible life stream. Tao, generally considered to be *"The Way"* is the Chinese word for the great sound, the Shabd.

THE UNIQUENESS OF SOUND

Our bodies are cascading fountains of energy systems, magnificent beyond imagination, and each one is entirely unique.

You may look and sound like other people but You are special. You carry a distinguishing energy, reflected in every muscle, every bone, every organ, every gland, every cell in your body.

Although we are all part of the Universal energy system, each man, each woman is different. Unique.

Think about it. The way you see things, think, react, love, are all a combination that makes you different. Corporations, product marketers, insurance agents and government lawmakers like to put us all in boxes because it gives them confidence.

THE BODY IS LIKE AN ORCHESTRA

In normal, healthy times your body should be like an orchestra playing beautiful music. It is wonderful. Then one day, something happens. A member of your orchestra starts feeling unwell and begins playing off key. Soon every part of the orchestra is affected and the entire unit struggles to exist. Until the one musician gets well, the orchestra is still out of whack. It's much like retuning a piano. A key that is off will scar the performance.. This is like the human body.

One small part affected by negative energy - an imbalance – will have an effect on the whole body. That imbalance can be changed with the use of sound.

Dr. Jenny and various researchers quickly discovered the power of sound in re-balancing the energy of the human body. It was also discovered that ancient teachers and practitioners used sound to rebuild health. But they did not call it energy. They had the concept of Sacred

Sound. To the ancients sound was and still is sacred. As we walk the Healing Paths we will talk about it.

WELCOME TO SOUND HEALING

Sound is an energy that can influence or change the vibrations of other energies . It influences and creates the correct natural resonant frequency of the part in the body that is out of tune. This causes it to vibrate back to its normal healthy state.

Here's what Sound Healing does:

It provides fast and deep states of relaxation.
It improves mental clarity and brain functioning.
It relieves stress by realigning the body into a centered space.
It boosts vitality and stamina.
Reduces or eliminate pain and discomforts.
Improves study habits and creativity.
Creates a healthy sense of wellbeing.

THE STRUCTURE OF SOUND

Sound consists of Pulse, Wave and Form. The pulse is the frequency, the wave is the part that has positive and negative forms, and the form is the amplification. Air carrying the sound is constantly being compressed and depressed.. That is why you can sometimes physically feel deep bass notes at a concert.

SOUND INSTRUMENTS

If you sit in a room with a clock (or a metronome) that is ticking every second, and your regular pulse is say seventy two, you will find that after about ten or fifteen minutes your pulse rate will have dropped to about sixty beats a minute. This is called entrainment. The cells of your body are coming into alignment with a sound outside your body.

Ticking clocks are great for inducing relaxation, but there are better, more fascinating ways of using sound. In sound healing there is a veritable array of sound making instruments. They range through such things as Tuning Forks, Otto Tuners, Celestial Tuners, ancient Singing Bowls, Tingshas, Didgeridoos, Rain Sticks, Native Indian flutes, Wuhan gongs, all with sounds that have the potential to realign the Elements of the Human Body. A sound healer works with many of these instruments.

THE POWER OF TUNING FORKS

Tuning forks play a significant role in sound healing. A tuning fork is an acoustic resonator in the form of a two-pronged fork that resembles the letter U, and it's made of elastic metal such as steel or aluminum. You may have seen a piano tuner at work with a tuning fork. When tapped , the fork vibrates and resonates at a specific constant pitch, and emits a pure musical tone. There are eight musical notes in an octave, and tuning forks are made for each note. Most sound healers use a set of tuning forks.

TAKING A COMSIC BATH

An interesting and effective relaxation technique is found with tapping two tuning forks simultaneously. Find yourself a quiet place where you will not be disturbed. Sitting with the tuning forks laid out before you.

Pick up the C-fork, get it vibrating and hold it close, but not touching your left ear. At the same time pick up a G-fork and have it vibrating close to your right ear. Now, listen to the joint or combined sound in your head.

When they have faded out of your audibility range, change the C-fork to your right ear, and get an A-fork vibrating in your left ear. When complete, replace the A-fork with an F-fork. Complete the meditation with the ones you started with – C and G forks. Student of music will recognize the Perfect Fifth.

In other words the set up should be like this: C – G, C - A, C – F and back to C – G.

To complete the exercise, hold the three forks – F, G and A in one hand, spaced between fingers so they are not touching, and strike all three with the C-fork. While they are all "singing" wave the forks around your body. Do this several times to feel the benefits of the sound.

Dr. John Beaulieu of www.biosonics.com and author of *Music and Sound in the Healing Arts* calls this useful exercise a *Cosmic Bath.* It is very relaxing and helps one to concentrate. I normally perform the Cosmic Bath before doing mediumship or giving a talk. It's also a good introduction to sacred sound. Through the exercise of tapping two tuning forks together, you have an introduction to sacred ratios.

SHARING THE VIBRATIONS

In sound healing it is useful to understand the Theory of Resonance. If you strike middle C on a piano, all the other Cs on that piano, and other musical instruments in the room will vibrate. It's like an echo. The C notes call out to each other. The same applies to any musical note. If two objects possess identical frequencies and one is vibrated, the other object will vibrate too. It's an offshoot of the Law of Cause and Effect. For every action there is an equal reaction.

Each cell in our bodies, and there are billions of cells, resonate to particular sounds. This is beyond the realms of known music. When a cell or a collection of cells falls out of tune and become sick, the task is to bring them back into their optimal functioning vibration. That is the object of sound healing.

Your pendulum will tell you where a problem is in your body, and the pendulum will also indicate which instrument would be best in getting those cells back into working order. This is why sound healers rely on a variety of instruments such as those mentioned above. If you do not possess a pendulum, use your intuitive powers. I feel that all healers should be equipped with pendulums.

THE POWER OF INTENT

One secret to good sound healing is intent. The intention is to heal a problem or a situation, therefore you focus and you concentrate. Whether you are healing a client, a friend or yourself, the intent to heal must be dominant and therefore one must remain focused. Allow yourself to become immersed with the sound and become part of it.

Harold Smith, a larger than life African-American came over to our Westville, New Jersey center to give us a lesson in the Australian didgeridoos. If you have never heard a didgeridoo, it produces a haunting drone. Harold brought several instruments along and among them was a large *"didge"* made of the Agave plant. It produced an unbelievably low drone, a super deep bass, and both Betty Lou and I felt the sounds in our lower abdomens. It brought tears to my eyes. You can hear Harold Smith on the CD *The Valley of Sacred Sound.*

Some people suggest the didge's drone is a mantra within the audible sound current, and I am positive this is so. The agave plant takes 25 years to bloom, and then promptly dies, and it is then that the shrub is used for such things as a didgeridoo, although most didges are made from eucalyptus trees.

Another powerful instrument in sound healing is the Wuhan gong. The big ones, 30 inches and more make rich sounds and you may spot one at the back of a large orchestra. We were introduced to sound healing by my sister Diane Egby Edwards, a professional sound healer in England. She had Betty Lou and myself stretched out on a floor mattress in her spiritual center in Bournemouth and performed a ten minute gong meditation. It was unbelievably powerful and every cell in our bodies seem to resonate to the deep rich sounds of the gong. In a few minutes our bodies were full of restored energy with a new awareness of Sacred Sound.

INSTRUMENTS ARE PERSONAL

Upon our return to the United States, we became certified sound healers and invaded Steve Weiss Music in Willow Grove, Pennsylvania. We spent several hours listening to the gongs before buying two large gongs which we use in our sound healing sessions. As with most instruments to be used for sound healing one has to listen and tune in to the sounds emanating. It's very much a personal decision.

The thing about all these sound healing instruments is they have little or nothing to do with traditionally structured music, and this includes the Native Indian flute, which is a great relaxer for the player and the listener. The flute is pentatonic which means there are five holes and the player creates his or her own sounds as they go along. Once you have breath control, you can create your own "works" or "compositions."

There are some great Native Indian flautists such as R. Carlos Nikai, Travis Terry, Odell Borg and John Two-Hawks. Whether you play or simply listen, go with the flow and allow the sounds to merge with all parts of your body. Native Indian flute music is excellent for healing. Drop by the Native Indian Arts and Crafts website at www.native-languages.org/flutes.htm. You will find a lot of useful information. Be careful when purchasing "Native Indian flutes" because as the website says, not all such flutes are crafted by Indians.

We have discussed various instruments that can be used for sound healing, except one, and that is the greatest sound instrument of all, the human voice.

YOUR VOICE HAS POWER

"Can you heal my neck?" It was a pleading call from the front row. We were at Parastudy, the Paranormal Research Center at Chester Heights near Philadelphia, Pennsylvania, discussing the phenomena of sound healing and in particular toning.

I had just said: "The most powerful instrument on earth is the human voice. Ironically, most people have never been taught to use their vocal healing powers, in fact, many people have been told, as children, to be quiet.

"Your voice can heal," I told the audience of about fifty. *"Your voice can heal,"* was a challenge, throwing down the old proverbial gauntlet.

"Can you heal my neck?" A pale, delicate and tiny lady, a senior citizen sitting in the front row held up her hand.

We promptly pulled over a chair and asked the lady to sit on it so everyone could see her. *"Focus on the discomfort in your neck and shoulders and give me a sound – it's a sound that your higher self says will heal your affliction."*

The lady thought for a moment, then made a sound between a prolonged *"eeeeee"* and an *ah-yeeeee."*

I asked her to take a comfortable, deep breath and make the sound as a continuous drone. Then I accompanied her and asked the audience to join in too. The room soon vibrated to the sound, and one could feel the energy bouncing around the woman and the room. We maintained the drone for about four minutes, then stopped.

The little lady was all smiles. "It's gone! " She wriggled her head in all directions. "It's really gone. I won't have to take asprin anymore."

Toning is a powerful part of sound healing. It uses the human voice. Most sound healers, including myself, train people in the use of toning. Effective toning can be learned in the space of an hour and the interesting part is, you have the opportunity not only to heal others, but yourself as well. Once you become adept you can keep your body, mind and spirit in balance. Stay tuned, we will show you how.

BE SEEN AND NOT HEARD, THEY SAID.

We still live in a world where children are told to keep quiet or told bluntly to "shut up." The noise kids make can be frustrating for adults under the rigors and pressures of stress. Negative reactions by grown-ups can seriously affect children for many years, including their adult life.

Perhaps you recall when you were a high-spirited child sounding off at the meal table and a parent rebuked you with the traditional *"Little boys and girls should be seen and not heard."* Sometimes, the rebuke might be a blunt *"Shut up! No one wants to hear your voice,"* or *"If you don't shut up you'll be grounded."* If such things were said once there would be no problem, but if such orders were familiar rebukes from a parent and repeated many times over the months and years, the message would sink deeply into the youngster's subconscious mind.

As we discussed earlier in self-talk, the subconscious mind learns through repetition, and in this particular situation it sits as a downside of the human system.

In business management the fear of public speaking is rampant. People know all there is to know about their businesses and would like to get out and lead seminars, give lectures and even appear on television, but they have a fear. It's called glossophobia. It affects many people. A well-known medical doctor once told me: *"I have to do a series of seminars and I'm terrified."*

During the consultation with the doctor and talking with various other clients, many confirmed that their parents had drummed it into their heads as children, *"Little children should be seen and not heard."* Little did the well-meaning parents then realize serious limitation it was placing on their children. It was a learning they could have done without. Some might even say it was voice abuse.

Of course, there are other occasions where childhood voices were suppressed. A child innocently touches a hot stove and starts screaming. The parent reacts: *"Stop crying. Big boys don't cry,"* or to a girl *"Stop crying. Do you ever see mother crying like that."* Perhaps you were told these sorts of things so many times, that when you grew up, when something hurt you, you kept the pain in. You suppressed the urge to cry. Bad! Crying is sound healing!

If ever you are hurt let the negative energy out. Scream, shriek, curse, shout, yell, groan, holler, squawk, squeal, yelp. It's nature's way of healing! You'll be glad you did.

LETTING GO OF INHIBITIONS

If you're a singer in any mode – opera, church choir, rock, middle-of-the road stuff, you should not have much difficulty in toning, although toning has nothing to do with music. It's being able to make sounds that may seem totally irrational—yet they have the power to heal. It's like magic.

To unload any inhibitions you may possess about using your voice, find a place where you will not be disturbed, or where people around you understand what you are doing.

EXERCISE: LETTING GO: Make yourself comfortable in an upright chair, hands unclasped on your lap, feet side by side. Now, take in a good, deep breath and let it out with a sigh! **A prolonged noisy sigh.** Do it again, and as the sigh is flowing out of your body, imagine you are letting go of any stresses, tension and inhibitions. Do this until you feel comfortable.

Next, make any sound that your inner self feels like making, It may be any or all of these sounds. **Whine, groan, growl, howl, squall, yelp, scream, shriek, grunt and so on.** Create any sound that makes you feel good right now. Keep it up for several minutes, then stop, be quiet and observe how your feel. This is one part of toning, there is a more systematic method of toning coming up.

Meanwhile, if you cannot find a place at home to do the above exercise, your car or truck, with windows closed is the next best place. Drive round the block and park somewhere that is quiet. Incidentally, you can perform toning in cars while driving through large cities where traffic is noisy and people are too busy to pay attention.

THE MAGIC OF VOWELS

Remember how our English teachers taught us that the 26-letter English alphabet is made up of vowels and consonants? The teacher probably told you that the terms vowel and consonant refer to the sounds which make up the spoken language. Vowels are open sounds and consonants are relatively closed. And that was that.

Perhaps, what the English teacher failed to tell you and me is that the five vowels in our alphabet have individual powers, especially when chanted or toned.

The five vowels in the alphabet. A - E - I - O - U.

Each vowel, sounded as a continuous drone without melody, without words, will have an impact or influence on a particular section of your body. It's simple and powerful, and if you have healthy vocal chords you can do it. One of the appealing aspects of toning is it costs nothing except some time and effort and it works like magic.

EXERCISE: TONING WITH VOWELS: Sit comfortably in an upright chair, hands on your lap, feet side by side. Close your eyes, take a deep breath and gently sound a prolonged *"You."* It will be like a stretched out *"YOUOOOOOOOOO."* The sound will not be high pitched, in fact it will be quite low. When you are out of breath, take another deep breath and continue. Do this for a couple of minutes. Then stop.

Where did you feel the sound influencing your body? If you did it correctly, it will have been in the area of the lower part of the body: hips, stomach, the pelvic area, legs and feet.

Before you start with the rest of the vowels, here's a tip: Start each vowel with a "huh" breathing sound.

- **Vowel I:** Pronounced *"EYE-EEEEEEEEE..."* It will impact the area of the head cavity. It will feel quite shrill and highly pitched.
- **Vowel E:** Pronounced *"EEEEEEEEEEEE..."* This will affect the throat and the lower chest areas. It will be less shrill than Vowel I.
- **Vowel A:** Pronounced *"AHHHHHHHHHHH..."* This will affect the chest cavity, lungs, heart, upper back and the upper body in general.
- **Vowel O:** Pronounced as an open *"OHHHHHHHHH..."* This effects the human torso, the trunk and the area from the solar plexus (belly button) to your groin.

When you have spent a few minutes toning each vowel, you will have an impression of how sound can be used in healing yourself and others. It is always a good idea at first to start experimenting on yourself.

CREATING SPECIAL SOUNDS

Once you have the concept and the power of the vowels, you can use them as a basis for all toning. Sometimes your higher self will suggest a mingling or merging of two or three vowels, and you may well surprise yourself at the tone that comes out.

As we did with the lady with the neck problem at ParaStudy, resort to asking the higher self to suggest a sound which will be appropriate for healing a specific condition. Remember, your higher self is that part of you that is in touch with God, the Universal Mind. It will be the sound that heals and it may sound quite strange.

Jonathan Goldman in his workshops and recorded programs creates a fabulous "NNNNGONG" which merges to "NNNNGANG" and goes to a "NNNNGING." As he produces this ongoing tone for several minutes, his hands direct the healing to the person in need of healing. He describes the process in detail in his book *Healing Sounds: The power of Harmonics*. It's an excellent exercise for manipulating the shape of the mouth, thus the healer as well as the healee benefits.

TONING IS A HEALING DRONE

No melody, no words, no rhythm, and no harmony, just the sound of the vibrating breath. It is a simple yet powerful technique, accessible to everyone regardless of vocal ability or training. Through toning you can immediately experience the effects of sound on your physical, mental, emotional, and spiritual well-being. Toning is a drone and it may sound peculiar, but it can heal beautifully.

Like all healing, the operator, in this case, the toner, must have positive intent and, of course, the intent is to heal.

If you have an ache or a muscle that is causing some degree of discomfort, even a stomach ache, or a leg muscle suffering cramps, practice the toning. Experimentation is important, because you will find your own strengths in this healing modality.

Always remember, you are sending a sacred sound, a healing message. Be responsible and remember to thank the Universe, the Cosmos, Infinite Intelligence for your ability and gift. And have fun. Whoever said that life was supposed to be grim and miserable was nuts!

EXERCISE: PRACTICE TONING: Sit in a straight chair, hands on your lap, feet together and focus on a condition in your body. It might be anything from a muscle ache, indigestion, eyestrain, itchy skin to something more serious, chronic arthritis to back pains and so on.

If it involves pain and can be measured, on a scale of zero to ten, ten being maximum discomfort and zero being pain free, make a note of your discomfort level before you start. Then after a treatment, check your discomfort level again. If you find the answers hard to get, use your pendulum.

Now, focusing on your condition, ask your higher self to come up with a sound that you can use for healing. Simply allow that to happen.

Remember, the intent is to heal. So, take a deep breath and sound the tone suggested by your higher self. Keep sounding that tone for about four minutes, then take a rest. Be in a relaxed or meditative state. Then sense your body. How does it feel? Better? You may need two or more sessions later. A toning session should not last for more than five minutes.

If you are working on a relative or friend who may be suffering from a condition, ask them to come up with a sound.You may wish to have a pre-session chat and explain the use of vowels in healing, and how successful you have been. If they are reticent in coming up with a vowel or a tone, tune in to your higher self and suggest one to them. Then get the person to sound it. This will be like an ice-breaker. You will discover exactly what I was writing about earlier – people are afraid to use their voices.

It's a good thing that Joshua had an enthusiastic set of people with fine voices (and horns) to bring down the walls of Jericho.

13

COLORS AND
POWER CENTERS

A S WE MENTIONED EARLIER, the human body contains a number of power centers. Depending on who you talk to they can range in number from seven to a hundred or more. They are called chakras, and for the sake of this discussion we will deal with the traditional seven power centers.

1ST CHAKRA: This is the base or Root power center at the bottom of your spine. It is the center that keeps you grounded, influences the adrenals, and the toning sound is "HUH." Make it as low as you can get it. Almost like a dog's growl.

2nd CHAKRA: This is the Sacral power center that influences the gonads and the ovaries and also the body's irrigation system. The toning sound is HOOOO, just like the hoot of an owl.

3rd CHAKRA: This is the Solar Plexus and it governs the digestive and respiratory functions of the body. In metaphysical terms it empowers your intuition, your ability to feel the joys and discomforts of others. Clairsentience is the psychic term. The toning sound is HOH much like a Santa Claus greeting but prolonged or in slow motion.

4th CHAKRA: This is the power center for the Heart and it governs the thymus. The heart chakra is midway between heaven and earth, because below are the physical power centers, and above are the spiritual centers. A well balanced heart center is important for any healer. The toning sound is an HAH, much like a cry of success "Ha, I told you so!" but prolonged.

5th CHAKRA: This is the Throat center which governs the thyroid, and in metaphysical terms clairaudience, the voices of higher self and spirits, and also inspirational speaking. The tone for this is HAY which comes over like "Aye, Aye" or "High."

6th CHAKRA: This is the Brow or third-eye power center, and traditionally it empowers the pituitary and pineal glands to create a psychic bridge. It is for the development of clairvoyance, psychometry and the seeing of spirits. The tone for this is EEE.

7th CHAKRA. This power center known as the Crown, sits on the top of your head. It influences the pineal gland. Some people consider this chakra as a direct link to God or the Cosmos, or both. The tone for this is a high sounding, very narrow EEEEE.

As you will readily realize by using different tones or a combination of tones one can balance the chakras, and regenerate any power center that may need healing. Before you begin, measure the effectiveness or health of each individual chakra with your pendulum. A chart, graded from zero to ten, showing positive and negative values is useful in measuring chakra effectiveness.

THE COMPLETE SOUND

This sound exercise covers the entire body, and is very effective if you do not know exactly where the problem exists in the body.

Tom Kenyon, director of Acoustic Brain Research in Washington State discovered that if a person has an out of balance acupuncture meridian, a healing sound will go to that meridian and correct the balance regardless of where the healing sound is being directed by the healer. That's powerful stuff.

Make sure you and the healee are grounded. Say a prayer for guidance, strength and protection to whoever you pray to. Have the person being healed recline on their back, head on a pillow.

Jonathan Goldman calls this technique *"The Siren,"* and you will soon understand the logic behind this title. The technique is so powerful that the person being treated may become light-headed.

Have the healee perform the complete breath several times with the breath going down to the diaphragm.Deep breathing will relax the person. Keep in mind your intent to heal, therefore know and respect the fact you are using sacred sound which is coming through you, and not of you.

Now, start with the very highest sound you can make, perhaps a shrill HEEEEE which impacts the head, and remembering the vowels from earlier, work down through the body and allow the sound to change from a high EEEEE to a very low, earthy HUUUUU, the deepest sound you can possibly make. Once you have reached the depths of the HUUUU start to climb up again to the shrill HEEEE. It will sound like a siren. Do it as slowly as you can.

Some people like to do the reverse, which is the method described by Laurel Elizabeth Keys in her book *Toning.* It's whatever works for you. Whichever way you decide, perform the Siren several times. Incidentally, you should practice this technique privately and get used to the prolonged breathing before healing another person.

After several scans you may find your toning is drawn to a particular part of the body. Allow your higher self to guide you and perform whatever sound is right. It is intuitive, metaphysical, spiritual. Continue toning until your higher self and your voice decides to stop. You will realize as you do so that you have been in a state of trance, perhaps Alpha, perhaps Theta.

Have the healee, the target rest for a few minutes with eyes closed, then ask them gently to talk about their feelings and describe any body changes. Encourage them to be open, and be open yourself in your sharing.

If you have performed on yourself, rest with your eyes closed and review your thoughts and feelings.

A HEALING CIRCLE WITH TONING

Perhaps you recall my earlier story of how, in a presentation on sound healing at Parastudy in Pennsylvannia, we gave sound healing to the little lady with the neck problem and the audience joined in with the toning? Well you can do it too, if you have a meditation group or a home church group.

Have the group sit in a circle, like a meditation or a message circle, and have the person who desires healing, to sit in the center of the circle. Say a prayer of protection and ask the group to tune into the Cosmos, the Universe, the Universal Mind and ask to be a medium for the transmission of Sacred Sound.

It is a good idea to have a spiritual warm-up by toning the OM or AUM mantra which symbolizes the Universal Mind and God.

An excellent way of toning AUM is to start with lips closed and sound a HUM. Then without stopping start to open the mouth slowly and keep sounding through HAAAAH until the mouth is full open and HOH is sounded. Then gradually close again slowly to an HUM. It may take half a minute so make sure everyone has taken a deep breath to begin. Sound the OM or the AUM for a few minutes.

USING COLOR IN TONING

The leader of the group then asks the person to be healed what sound comes to mind for their healing, or if it is difficult to come up with a sound, ask for a color that represents healing to them.

If they say RED, the Sacred Sound is UH. Here are some others. ORANGE is HU, YELLOW is OH, GREEN is AH, BLUE is AY, INDIGO is EE and Violet is MMM or OM.

The group may well start off with the Sacred Sound suggested by the healee and the Group MIND will take over and change it to a more appropriate tone for the healee. It's somewhat amazing how Spirit works. There is no fixed time for toning for an individual sitting in a circle, but the leader will sense that it is time to stop.

With permission of the healee a discussion can take place afterwards on how the person felt during the session. What parts of his/her body were impacted? Did they feel hot or cold? Did they experience a dream. Did they clairvoyantly "see" any entities? Group or Communal Toning is a learning experience for both the healee and members of the circle.

SPIRITS ATTRACTED BY GROUP TONING

Circle or Group Toning is very attractive to visiting spirits. Often they are loved ones and relatives who have departed into the Spirit World. Sometimes they are spirits who are just plain curious, attracted by the sounds and are attending with a view to learning.

Sound healing is such a powerful modality, that participants in the circle may well start to see visiting spirits clairvoyantly, or hear spirits clairaudiently or feel spirits clairsentiently, or a combination of all three. It does happen.

Even individual toning sessions will often attract spirits of loved ones. It's almost as if a flag goes up on the Astral Plains and friends and relatives drop down and observe the proceedings.

My writing guide Paul says when people start toning it creates an attractive red presence in the Spirit World.

When holding group toning the advice is be prepared for visitors and messages. This why one starts with a prayer calling for guidance, strength and protection. Enjoy!

14

GUIDES, ANGELS
AND HELPERS

THEY ARE KNOWN AS SPIRIT GUIDES, guardian angels, spirit helpers, astral teachers and some folk still refer to them as goddesses. Goddesses is probably an imprint from past lives or some bio-psychological influence buried deep in that so-called "junk" DNA that scientists are still trying to figure.

A lot of people have been consciously influenced by spirits, and all people, at some time or another, have been consciously or unconsciously influenced by spirits from the astral states.

They come in all shapes and sizes. My first encounter with a spirit occurred when at the tender age of six, I was bedbound with a then fatal blood disease called septicemia. The doctor, making a house call in 1939 bluntly informed my mother, *"I don't think there is much hope for Bobbie. He's going to die."* A few minutes after they had departed my bedroom, a lady, a shimmering, silvery being in white appeared. She informed me flat out: *"You're not going to die, Bobbie. You will get well."* No ifs ands or buts. You will get well!

Then she faded, and I do not recall ever "seeing" her again but I did feel she was around. And I still do, and I do not even know her name. I recall her voice, a slight husky voice. I have a distinct feeling that she will be back and I will discover her name. In the meanwhile I simply refer to her as "Her."

A DIRECT LINK WITH GOD

We all have guardian angels, whether we like it or not. They are our direct link with God, the Universal Mind, the Creator. They are a string. A connector. How this works is something beyond our comprehension, because if the Universal Mind is part of us, where is the need for a link?

Paul says the guardian's function is to prevent or deter negative energies from invading our weakened bodies and minds during the sleep process. During this sleep function, the spirit frequently leaves the body, travels, learns and makes contact with other entities. The guardian stays in charge of the sleeping form.

Occasionally you can see your guardian angel. Here's how. As you return from sleep to waking consciousness, lie on your back with eyes closed, so that to all intents and purposes you are still asleep. Keep your body motionless, then suddenly open your eyes and look straight up above. If you are fast, you will see a flash of white light, almost like lightning, and a split second later it will be gone. Your guardian has just gone off duty.

The guardian is also your life guide, sometimes influencing when the need arises, but rarely, if ever communicating directly.

A life guide will activate your intuitive faculties, and trigger a little voice that says "Watch out!" supposedly to enable you to avoid a major accident or incident.

BULLETS IN THE BEDROOM

When I was a news photographer and correspondent in the turbulent Middle East, there were many times when the little voice warned me or alerted me to avoid something. It was an era before I had conscious awareness of metaphysics or intuitive powers.

During the Lebanese civil war of 1958 I was working for United Press and staying in the Hakim Hotel in Tripoli, an oil port in northern Leba-non. The armed conflict was Christian Arabs versus Moslem Arabs. In those days the President was Christian and the Prime Minister, Rashid Karameh was Moslem. The city of Tripoli was divided and the Hakim

Hotel was in the Christian sector and overlooked the Old City. There was a dividing line between the two forces and every night at about nine, the city erupted into a blaze of bombs and bullets, which normally lasted for two or three hours.

The moslems had an interesting method of delivering bombs. They would strap explosives inside a car or truck tire, and then set the detonator. Like children playing with hoops, they would run the tire-bombs down a dark, narrow alley and send them hurtling across the broad street dividing the city and into the Christian sector where they would explode.

Nights were normally quite quiet after about eleven and one could get a peaceful night's sleep.

But one day it was barely dawn. The light of a new day was seeping over the hills east of the city. My room faced east and I always appreciated a beautiful dawn sky...until the voice hissed in my head: "Roll out of bed. Do not stand up. Roll against the far wall, under the washbasin."

I had heard the voice before. It was Her. I rolled off the bed and across the room to the far wall. Not a moment too soon. The ripping sound was more like a cannon shot going through my room than a bullet. It was loud and deadly.

Machine-gun fire sprayed the Hakim Hotel. It felt like an eternity, but Prime Minister Rashid Karameh told me later that morning it was, in fact, only thirty seconds. Karameh was the perennial prime minister of Lebanon. A pure gentleman and one of the nicest lawyers I ever met.

"It was a Hotchkiss," he said with a smile and a shrug. In World War One the Hotchkiss was the standard machine-gun of the French Army who had occupied Lebanon from 1920 to 1946 and a substantial number or arms were left behind. *"One of my men, an enthusiastic fighter, observed the United Nations flag on the roof of the Hakim and tried to shoot it down. My apologies for the inconvenience. Come and have breakfast."*

It was true, the United Nations Peace Force had arrived the night before and had set up their base in the Hakim Hotel and during the night had hoisted the U.N. flag atop the building.

Upon reflection, it was the second time in two days that the voice had whispered warnings. The other time was on the Lebanese/Turkish border when I narrowly averted walking on a landmine, which I described in "The Quest of the Radical Spiritualist." One of these days, I need to write my memoirs of my days as a journalist and news photographer in the company of such notables as Larry Collins, Joe Alex Morris, Larry Burrows, Ralph Izzard, Russell Jones and others. Some twenty-nine years later in 1987 when I was in far off Canada, I heard that the highly respected Rashid Karameh had been assassinated.

Whether you believe or not in guardian spirits, their voices are helpful to stay alive and healthy.

THE BELIEF IN SPIRITS?

An incredible number of Americans believe in spirits and angels. More than half of all adults, fifty-five per cent, believe that they have been protected by a guardian angel during their life. This was according to a 2008 survey by Baylor University's Institute for Studies of Religion. The survey polled 1,700 respondents of diverse religious faiths: evangelical Protestants, black Protestants, mainline Protestants, Catholics and Jews. It is a phenomenon that crosses religious as well as regional and educational lines.

Some sources believe these figures are actually higher than the poll reveals, because a lot of people are quite fearful of expressing their feelings and experiences when it comes to contact with the occult. But what is occult?

People love to bandy words such as "occult" not really understanding what they truly mean. In a nutshell, it means "hidden." So the next question is: "Can you see God?"

When asked workshops, most people respond in the negative. Some will even say that God is hidden. Therefore, logically, God must be part of the occult. That is, unless you can see God. As we will discuss later, God is within and without, and very much in evidence.

When it comes to angels and spirit guides always remember the teachings. In this case recall Psalm 91, verses 11 and 12: *"His angels are given charge of you, to guard you in all your ways. On their hands they will bear you up, lest you dash your foot against a stone."* That sums up the work of a guardian angel. Know you have one and enjoy.

SPIRIT GUIDES AND HELPERS

Like people in your life, loved ones, career and social friends, your relationships are governed by the Universal Law of Attraction. And so it is with spirit guides, and entities from the Other Side. Remember the old adage: *"Birds of a feather flock together."* Well in spiritual terms it manifests itself as *"like attracts like."* You attract into your life only those people who match your energy vibration, and are on your wavelength, so to speak. Take a few moments now to think about the people you have attracted into your life, or those close about you. Observe impartially what sort of people they also attract into their lives.

It is the same with your spirit guides, teachers and helpers. Your spirit teachers will match your vibrations, because they are all governed by the powerful Law of Attraction. You may find a spirit guide just comes into your life with no ringing of bells or big announcements. The newcomer simply shows up very quietly and starts helping you.

This happened when I was studying healing and hands-on-healing with mediums Patrick Young and Isabel Corlett in Vancouver many moons ago. Isabel casually mentioned one day: *"Bob, there's a little Chinese fellow wandering around after you. He says he's here to help with your healing."*

As I mentioned previously Chang, a doctor in Imperial China, crossed over in 1893, He joined me in 1978 and he is still working with me after thirty years. It was Chang who taught me astral protocol which comes under the Law of Life. Apparently you do not ask your current spirit teacher to put you in touch with a new spirit guide. You ask Infinite Intelligence, God, Holy Spirit, your Creator, the Source of Your Being and so on. You ask whoever you pray to. My favorites are Holy Spirit and Universal Mind. God does not mind what name you use, just call and speak.

GETTING A SPIRIT GUIDE

In your Sanctuary of the Mind state your request to God. *"Holy Spirit, I wish to develop and use my intuitive and healing abilities, and I would greatly benefit from being assigned a spirit teacher, a spirit guide. If this is your will, allow this to happen. Thank you."* Nothing ostentatious, simply state the facts. If you need a spirit guide to assist with healing, medium-ship, spiritual studies, automatic writing, inspirational speaking, say so, but keep it simple.

Some New Age gurus might advise you to doctor the words with oodles of niceties. Resist, and know that that is pure ego-chatter, and the Radical Spiritualist refrains from False Self chatter.

Also, recall the words that Jesus, the master healer taught us: *"Your Father in Heaven knows what you want even before you ask."* Just state your requirement, plain and simple. Once you have filed your request, expect to hear or realize the presence of a special spirit teacher in your life.

DESIRE IS THE FUEL FOR ACTION

One extremely valid point: You must possess a real desire to meet a spirit guide. Desire is the fuel for getting things done, and it is good to have a vision. Why do you want an active spirit guide in your life? In anything you do, it is of paramount importance that you have an objective, a vision. If it's in line with the purpose of this book, that is exploring healing paths for self development, then you need to have some objectives.

As you will have read by now, the healing path of the radical spiri-tualist traverses a number of modalities, and there are many more we have not even touched. The Radical Spiritualist maintains an open mind and explores many different paths of healing before deciding on a special field.

It is possible that the healing guide you desire may serve your initial objectives to explore different fields of healing, and then as you special-ize or feel drawn to a particular path, your first guide will give way to a more specialized guide to assist you.

AN ALL-ROUND LEARNING OPPORTUNITY

Always remember, that serving a human being is an important learning function for the spirit guide. Do not get upset if a guide answers your question with *"I don't know, but I will find out."* Allow your spirit friends and teachers the opportunity to learn and move on.

The speed at which guides function and communicate is frequently mind-boggling. If they have to "find out," some information they may be gone for ten seconds, only to return and talk to you for fifteen or twenty minutes. They live and work at such a high vibration, you may well have to request your guide to *"slow down so I can hear and understand."*

EXERCISE: WHY I NEED A SPIRIT GUIDE

Find a place where you will not be disturbed. Have a writing pad and a pen or pencil. Play some relaxing music. Write down your experience or feelings about healing and living a healthy life. Are you interested in self-healing or becoming a healer to help others. At this stage how do you see your objectives?

The second part of this exercise: Write down some questions to put to your spirit guide when you meet him or her.

Practical experience has shown that many, if not most students, when they meet a spirit, appear to be dumb-founded. It's an old complaint: *"I didn't know what to ask."*

For starters, ask their name, and ask how they wish to be called. They may well tell you to *"Pick a name."* If they are in any way an ascended teacher, they may wish to keep their true identity shielded. It is the information they impart to you, the training that is important. You will recognize the truth as you progress.

GET INTO THE HABIT OF ASKING QUESTIONS

Not knowing their true name should not hamper you from asking questions. Work to get some background. Did you ever live on Earth? How many lives did you spend on Earth? How can you help me? What do you do in the Spirit World? Do you have a mentor? Get into the habit of asking questions. It will boost your knowledge and self confidence.

RESIST PATTERNS AND FOMULAE

One more thing, resist the desire to look for a formula or a pattern in healing. There are all sorts of books and gurus out there that spill out pages of ritualistic material they claim will make you a good healer.

The late author and lecturer Frank C. Tribbe in a paper printed in the Journal of The Academy of Religion and Psychic Research in July and October 1997, made a valid point on rituals. He pointed out that while Jesus, the healer gave instructions in his healing, there was no pattern.

There is *"no record that Jesus ever refused anyone who asked for a healing; He never said, 'If it is God's will'; there is no Beatitude for the sick; He never said ill health will further spiritual growth; He rarely mentioned faith; some never asked for a healing but were healed; goodness clearly was not necessary."*

It is apparent that one of the world's greatest healers had no set of spiritual laws, no cut-and-dried pattern to follow to ensure a return to health. It is safe to say, **Jesus of Galilee was a radical spiritualist.**

Now you should have some information and ideas for meeting an entity.

MEETING THE SPIRIT GUIDE

The easiest and most convenient place to meet a new spirit guide is in trance and in your special place, your Sanctuary of the Mind.

A number of successful first time encounters with spirit guides have been made by people, who simply pray to God and ask for a guide, then wait for someone to appear. In the Sanctuary of the Mind they may come across the lawn, or be spotted walking along the beach, or seen coming down the mountain trail. When you see a figure approaching it is easier to assimilate the details. No one really wants a spirit guide coming with the suddenness of a jack-in-the-box. If this technique of a gradual approach works, go ahead. It is the tried and tested method I gave in my book "The Quest of the Radical Spiritualist" and it is reproduced here in essence.

EXERCISE: THE BALL OF WHITE LIGHT: In your Sanctuary of the Mind envision a ball of the purest white light coming towards you, starting in the distance and slowly getting bigger. Make it as white as new fallen snow basking in beautiful sunlight.

Gaze into the white ball and expect to see a face. It may be young, perhaps old, it does not matter. It will smile but behind that smile is the wisdom of the ages. Once you have detected a face, mentally ask the spirit guide to join you. At this time, a tunnel of white light will open and your guide will walk towards you, either in physical form or as a light body.

Next step: Welcome your spirit guide. The entity will come in on a vibration of profound love that you may not have experienced before. Never try to compare it to Earthly love. It will be different, almost unexplainable. Allow it to happen. Give your newly arrived guide a hug. Know that you are lovable and huggable.

BE PATIENT AND CHAT

Take time to talk with your spirit guide. The entity may well be aware of your hesitation in asking questions, and may start talking and asking you questions.

In workshops I always suggest students create a list of questions to ask a newly arrived spirit guide. There can be many topics, many questions. Keep your mind open and answers will flow. At first you may feel you are imagining things, and that is all right. One day, something will happen to validate your encounter and this will confirm your rendezvous and confirm that spirits do exist. Exercise patience.

Finally, thank the spirit for this meeting, and allow the entity to recede into the ball of white light. You can follow this procedure until you feel confident and recognize the presence of your spirit guide when you are doing everyday things. When your relationship really blooms it will be like having a friend or a colleague at your side. (Right now as I write, Chang and Paul are floating around the room, adding comments and ideas.)

Some students often ask when will they get an invitation to enter the white light. It will happen when you are ready. There are many things to do, see and learn about the spirit world, but most guides will insist you further your healing education on the Earth plain before venturing to higher states.

ANOTHER WHITE LIGHT OPPORTUNITY

You may also find out while performing the Ball of White Light technique, that loved ones and friends in the Spirit World may come through. You need to ask: "I would love to meet a departed person from my life. If they are available, I would appreciate a rendezvous."

A loved one or friend may appear in the Ball of White Light, or they may simply materialize coming across the lawn, walking along the beach, or coming along a trail in the meadow. There is no fixed plan for encounters. Just allow them to occur and enjoy.

COMMUNICATING WITH SPIRITS

Spirit guides are a delight to work with and enjoy. When you have been communicating formally with your spirit guides for a while, you will find they start to communicate informally. Ideas simply pop into your head for no apparent reason, and then you realize that is part of your upcoming agenda. It's kind of spooky at first, but one does get used to it.

Whenever I meditate in my special place, my Sanctuary of the Mind, I always know if they have something they wish to discuss. As I enter the sanctuary, a beautiful and expansive garden, there are some white wicker seats surrounding a round wicker table. They are set in a shady cove of evergreen trees. When I arrive, if one or more of the guides are present, I know there is an agenda.

Today, as I write this they are suggesting I write a chapter near the end of the book on the "Audible Life Stream," or the "Shabd."

"I have this in mind," I respond enthusiastically. "I've had this in mind for some time. It will help radical spiritualists move to a higher level."

"Our thoughts entirely," murmured Paul with a short laugh. "Did you create the idea or did you hear it from us."

"Difficult to say," I admitted. Which was true.

"Where are you going now on the Healing Path? How about spirit rescue? That's something that needs publicizing," said Paul thoughtfully.

Chang added: "Spirit rescue! A great opportunity for healers to work with spirit guides and those spirits snagged in transition."

With a faked grimace I said: "You've been pushing this idea in my consciousness for quite a while."

"Who us?" Laughter rippled through my Sanctuary. It is always good when spirits laugh.

15

THE RELUCTANT
SPIRITUALIST

*Note: The following story actually happened in mid-October 2009,
and it demonstrates how well-intended spirits can influence a
scenario for a person over a period of months.*

PULL UP A PEW and lend an ear while I mull over some peculiar
happenings that occurred in New Mexico, the state beloved by
film-makers, artists, spies, atom bomb makers and throngs of
curious tourists who seek the Indian pueblos. The wide expanse of
desert, dotted with red cedar, the perfectly blue sky that attracted many
artists, including Georgia O'Keefe, appealed to my sense of finding a
place to meditate and ponder life, death, the Universe and everything.

When I first started at home in upstate New York of mulling over the
maps and booklets on Albuquerque and New Mexico, for some strange
reason I was drawn to a place called Socorro.

Socorro has been around for some 400 years and it sits in the Rio
Grande Valley, about 75 miles south of Albuquerque. A small City at
4,600 feet, it is surrounded by a number of extinct volcanoes. When it
comes to big bangs however, Socorro has had its share. A short 35 miles
away to the south-east at a place they called Trinity, humanity on July
16th 1945 detonated the first atomic bomb. It was a dress rehearsal for
ending World War Two and it ushered in a new era for the planet.

The bomb was transported to the site in what is now the White Sands Missile Range in a 200 ton steel container with walls 14 inches thick. A chunk of it survived and can be found on display on the Socorro plaza. If you place your hands on the chunk and perform psychometry you will receive powerful vibrations. My partner Betty Lou felt the vibrations through her body. I sensed two blasts, one initial small one, followed moments later by a tremendous blast. The chunk is still alive with memories well over half a century later.

Was this why I was drawn here? I didn't think so. One place I had hoped to see was the ruins of the old Kelly Mine, but I was really reluctant to drive another 30 miles on some questionable roads to see ruins that guide books said there was not much to see.

After wandering around Socorro and taking a coffee, I said to my partner Betty Lou: *"Not much here, let's get back to Albuquerque."* Well, it didn't happen. We felt an urge to talk to a lively lady in the City Tourism Bureau. She told us about an intriguing place called Magdalena tucked away in the Magdalena mountains, some 27 miles to the west of Socorro. Early Spanish settlers claimed to see the image of Mary Magdalene in the rockface of one of the mountains—when the sun is right. Curious, we drove to Magdalena but the sun wasn't right, so we drove around the small town, somewhat disappointed. In mid-October most places are closed. Magdalena was almost deserted of people, as if Gary Cooper was coming at High Noon. We observed an absence of street signs which was annoying. I felt an impatience to get out of town.

A SURPRISE FROM GPS

"Let's get back to Socorro and have lunch in the micro-brewery," I said. Well, instead of getting out of town immediately, our curiosity took us cruising through the residential area in the hope of spotting some local residents. Suddenly, my GPS told me where we were – on Kelly Road!

"It must be a sign," I told Betty Lou. "But heck, It's another five miles," There was no sign of my guides, and that was strange.

In spite of my growing reluctance we drove on. When the road changed to gravel, my reluctance escalated. If it had not been for my GPS

176

identifying the road, we certainly would have called it a day and returned to Socorro and Albuquerque. The uninviting road rapidly deteriorated and it kept on getting worse by the minute. I was worried about the car because it was a new rental from Enterprise.

Reaching the brow of a hill, we found a very old church with a sign "St. John the Baptist, Kelly N.M." It stood alone on a plateau like a sentinel, surrounded by steel fence. We parked the car and wandered around. The church is a gallant relic of the old community of Kelly, long since gone to dust. Still, services are held here once a year we discovered. There was no sight of the illusive old mine. It was like the guide books said, nothing much to see.

A YOUNG MAN ON A BICYCLE

Disappointed I stared at the heavily rutted track going up the mountain. It was probably too rough for any all-terrain vehicle, let alone our rental car.

"I'm not going any further," I told Betty Lou and she agreed we had simply had enough. We spotted a man on a horse in the distance. He looked like Clint Eastwood in one of those Italian westerns. He was too far away to hear us. Returning to the car I was about to start the engine when a young man on a bicycle appeared--almost out of nowhere.

He parked his bike against the church fence and unstrapped his helmet.

"The Kelly Mine? You're almost there. A quarter of a mile up the track." He said he lived "nearby" and had come from West Virginia some three years before.

"Could we hike up," I asked cautiously.

"Sure. It's just up the track. No problem." He seemed enthusiastic for us to go on.

Well, that quarter mile was the longest we had ever climbed. There were some distinct problems. That quarter mile is at an elevation well over 8,000 feet, so the oxygen is not as plentiful as at sea level. The track ran a steady incline over rough rocks. The sun beamed mercilessly out of a perfectly blue sky that would have made Georgia O'Keefe tremble in

177

ecstasy. It was burning at 80-degrees. Add to this the fact we had no water, and are both in our mid-seventies, and you have weird, if not hairy situation.

As we walked I kept telling myself, *"Egby your nuts! Why are you torturing your body like this? There's nothing to see."* Twice, our lungs felt seriously short of oxygen and we had to stagger over and rest under the shade of a red cedar. Finally, we reached the sign that proclaimed "Kelly Mine."

I told Betty Lou, "I'll just get some photos of the sign and we'll head back down. This is plain stupid. We should not have come."

A battered sign declared that visitors must acquire a pass in Magdalena if they wished to visit the mine. Ha! Now they tell us! I took some photos of the sign and the distant buildings by telephoto lens and was ready to turn back, totally unimpressed when something happened.

Voices! Not physical voices. Spirit voices. They came in softly at first, then their enthusiasm grew. "...hear us...he can hear us," one man's voice said it several times. "He thinks we're ghosts...that's what the others said...I think we should take cover..."

"Spirits!" I told Betty Lou. "There are spirits here." Suddenly, my exhausted body discovered the energy to walk through the gate into the works area. The old mine buildings and machinery stood brave but desolate in the scorching New Mexican sunshine. It seemed strange to think that in another age, spanning fifty years, that a whole community had lived here, mining lead, zinc, silver, copper, gold and later smithsonite. Production totaled over $30 million. There were hotels, saloons, stores, brothels, stables, homes, a school and offices. Kelly was a vibrant town and its focal point, its life giver, was a mine..

"What are they?" Betty Lou asked.

"Earth-bounds. They haven't crossed over."

A sudden chorus of spirit voices almost like boisterous children filled my space and I demanded they be quiet while I found a concrete wall on which to sit while I recovered from the climb.

Earth-bounds are spirits that have left their physical bodies upon so-called death and failed to make a full transition into the Spirit World. There are many reasons for this snag in transition. Some spirits simply do not want to leave the Earth plain, some do not believe there is a God and an Afterlife and struggle to stay. Some struggle to stay with loved ones or close friends. Others wish to retain their power they had on Earth. Others refuse to believe they are "dead" and struggle to stay on the Earth plain.

Soldiers get killed in wartime and are so conditioned, they sit around in spirit "waiting for orders" – orders that do not come. At the Kelly Mine, the voices sounded like miners.

"Who is in charge?"

An entity who had once been a shift manager, came forward. He called himself "Tom" and when I responded with *"Thomas"* he corrected me and insisted he was named *"Tom."* He had a vague Welsh accent.

"How many of you are there?"

"Eight," he responded promptly. Betty Lou working with a pendulum nodded. She had already dowsed the number.

I wanted to know how long they had been here.

"Ah, we've been here ever since the mine closed a few years back. We worked the mine and lived locally after she closed. Then most of us got sick and that's when funny things happened. Some of us said we were dead, others claimed we were dreaming. I don't know really. Are we dead? I don't feel dead, just sort of funny. I get terribly depressed at times and I like to find a quiet place down in the mine. It's like home."

The miners had obviously lost track of time. Tom's observation that the *"mine closed a few years back"* was in reality almost eighty years before. Earth-bounds are notorious for losing track of time, and can spend decades and even centuries wandering around repeating similar questions to visitors, particularly rock hunters who come by. Their favorite was: *"We are waiting for the mine to reopen. Any idea when this will be?"* No one ever answered because no one ever heard them. And if they did, they thought they were *"imagining things."*

Tom stared at me. "What's your name?"

"Bob. I do psychic stuff. Mediumship."

"Bob, tell us the truth, 'because truth is I think we're dead. Are we dead? Is this all there is?"

"No, you're not dead. Your bodies have been left behind, but you're as alive as I am. I can tell you some things."

For the next few minutes I told them about the Spirit World, Summerland, Heaven as some call it, and said they should all be there, not wandering around the ruins of the old Kelly Mine looking for work. *"There are loved ones, sweethearts, friends, who have gone on and are still waiting for you. They are all ready to help."*

Most of my communication was telepathic, which is the communication medium of spirits, but when I started talking about loved ones and sweethearts, the scene changed, as if someone had flicked a switch.

Warm, vibrant energy, more powerful than the heat of the sun came surging in. *"We've just been joined by a whole lot of angels..."* I said, noting the arrival of spirit helpers who said they brought miners' loved ones with them.

To Betty Lou I said: *"The miners can't see spirits from the spirit world because they are depressed and looking down."*

The old Kelly Mine, basking in the October sun, was suddenly a gathering of spirits, all ready to help the miners.

The problem with earth-bounds is they become victims of depression, and the challenge is getting them to look up, raise their vibration. After years of isolation, many mechanically look down, tuning into the earth. If only they would look up, workers from the spirit world would be able to assist them in crossing over without having to rely on spirit rescuers, like me in the physical. .

"Are you all ready to join your loved ones?" I asked Tom. He hesitated. "They're all discussing what's happening. Wait while I talk to them." Suddenly there was a quiet in the ranks, then he came back. *"It's time"* he said slowly. *"It's time to leave."*

I noted my spirit guides Paul and Chang were close by. In a prayer of protection to Holy Spirit, I asked for guidance, strength and protection and to open the way, the light for these miners to make their last journey home.

Then addressing the eight, I described the Summerland, the Spirit World and how it is a place where they can be free again, be with loved ones and friends, and advance in their spiritual lives. *"It's time to let go of the Earth, lift your heads and gaze up into the beautiful white light shining above you."* I mentally repeated these words several times and finally felt an upward movement – a vibration change -- within the group. *"The light is the gateway to your home,"* I told them. There were gasps among the miners. They had suddenly seen the spirits gathered round them.

"Go with the angels and loved ones. They will guide you all home." The heaviness that had existed around the miners started to clear. A few moments later, we knew that all eight had crossed over successfully.

Paul called out "All clear. Good job. Glad you came?"

Then I realized I had been used again. Ever since I had picked up the New Mexico magazine, maps and brochures some months before while sitting in upstate New York, and started reading about Socorro, Magdalena and the Kelly Mine, it was all predestined. I had been reluctant to come at all stages. Even our friends in Albuquerque had queried us going. I kept wanting to turn back, but it never happened. Even when we reached the Church of St. John the Baptist on the old Kelly Road, someone suddenly appeared on a bicycle and urged us to go on.

I vividly recalled a time years before when I was trekking to a Holy place called St. Just in Roseland in Cornwall, England. I had been hiking in England's west country and had reached a point of reluctance. I was tired and exhausted. Then, suddenly a boy on a bicycle appeared out of nowhere and urged me to go on, pointing to a rainbow in the sky. I wrote about it in "The Quest of the Radical Spiritualist." Coincidence?

"That young man at the church...on the Kelly Road...did you have anything to do with that?" I growled at Paul.

A peal of laughter seemed to echo around the old Kelly Mine site. "Robert, I'll never tell," cried Paul. "Cosmic secrets." Mystics have a saying: There are no such things as coincidences, only occurrences of energy we fail to understand."

As we walked down the rough track to the old St. John the Baptist Church, we stopped to look at the ruins, shells of buildings with 16-inch rock walls that had once been part of the mining community of Kelly, New Mexico.

The place still holds energies of bygone days. The akashic records are still strong. If you are quiet you may well hear the horses panting and coughing as they drag the ore-carts down the dusty track to Magdalena and the rail head. You can still hear the mine whistles, men walking home after shifts underground, women chatting, and children laughing.

In the eternal akashic records the old Kelly Mine is still very much alive, still working, still vibrating in time. We helped eight earth-bounds that hot autumnal day, October 17th 2009. I do have a strong feeling, there are more spirits still earth-bound lurking amid the mine ruins at 8,000 feet, still waiting for assistance, a rescue to get to their eternal home on the Other Side.

16

THE ULTIMATE HEALING: SPIRIT RESCUE

CCORDING TO THE World Health Organization statistics about 141,000 people die every day on Planet Earth, and for the most part, loved ones and friends believe they have "crossed over" into the Spirit World. They have "gone to Heaven" as most would say.

The problem is not all spirits cross over. A very small percentage fail to make the transition. For a variety of reasons that will become apparent, they fail to follow the spiritual path into the light to be welcomed on the "Other Side." To put it bluntly, they get snagged in transition.

The whole thing is steeped in metaphysics and there are not many scientists who have studied the problem. This is because scientists like to repeat hypotheses before they even consider declaring that a phenomenon has an element of truth, and it is very difficult to test something that you cannot see or at least control. Perhaps one day the technology will be available for accurate studies to be carried out.

CLINGING TO LIFE

How do earthbound spirits come about? How do they get snagged in transition? We touched on this in the previous chapter, but basically, it is because they do not wish to leave the presumed comforts or attractions of Planet Earth, or they do not believe there is an Afterlife.

It happens in a variety of cases. For instance, the person wishing to terminate his or her life, starts to take a drug overdose, then somewhere in the process, renegs, gets cold feet and says: "No, I don't want to end my life like this." The problem is the process has started and it is too late. The body has closed down. The spirit, fully conscious is out of the body, and feverishly clings to familiar people and places. They cling to familiar earthly haunts. Looking up into the Cosmic light above is unknowing. Its not the same as Earth, so they rarely if ever look up. Frantically they grasp for earthly things and people. Lovable, reliable, solid things.

There are two problems manifesting here. Loved ones, family and friends still at home are plunged into grief over the loss. A death is something highly stressful that most people find difficult to handle even at the best of times, such as when a sick person is expected to die. The death of a loved one prompts a total involvement in the loss. They have no time or thought for the earthbound spirit still around.

On top of this, most people, even at the best of times, do not use their intuitive or pyschic abilities, otherwise they would see and feel the unhappy spirit striving to make contact. And even if they do sense its presence, they will likely brush it aside and say: *"How silly. I am imagining things."*

BEING BRUSHED OFF!

Earthbounds attempt desperately to make contact with loved ones. They follow them around and try to communicate. Earthbounds have told me: *"That is the worst part, trying to get in touch with loved ones and being totally ignored. Brushed off. That hurts."*

The earthbound spirit becomes totally frustrated and depressed and seeks the comfort of places he or she remembers, warm, happy, reliable places. Over time, they become not only depressed, but their energy radiates coldness.

People with an earthbound spirit in the home will make such comments as "the back bedroom has suddenly become very cold, do you think we should have the heating checked?" or "the staircase feels very uncomfortable, almost as if someone was looking at me."

When a room or a part of the house mysteriously and for no apparent reason turns cold over a short period of time, it may well suggest the presence of an earthbound spirit. Good spirits, happy spirits who have crossed over into the Spirit World and are returning to old haunts, old friends and loved ones to check them out, normally leave a warm, positive feeling.

A developing coldness, in spite of places being heated are symptoms of a negative energy, and can be symptoms of an earthbound spirit.

REASONS FOR EARTHBOUND SPIRITS

Becoming earthbound can happen to a variety of people for a variety of reasons. There is no set pattern, no set of reasons, simply because each spirit that becomes earthbound has a unique personality, a unique consciousness, a unique set of beliefs.

The False Self, the ego, with all its many faces is still in existence when a spirit becomes earthbound. However, will systematically dissolve, sometimes rapidly when a spirit has made a full transition into the Spirit World. But as a human being approaches death for a variety of reasons, the False Self with its individual beliefs plays a major role in the transition and demise of the earthbound spirit.

It may happen to a chronically sick and dying person who adamantly refuses to believe in the existence of God and Heaven and who has distinct aversions to becoming "dust to dust" in the local cemetery. It might happen to young person who enjoyed a boisterous life full of thrills and excitement, but was killed in an auto accident, or a person who hanged himself in the home basement.

One earthbound spirit we helped cross over had died of cancer a few months before his grandchild was born, and he tried to cling to life to see and welcome the child. As an earthbound spirit, he would sit in the growing child's bedroom and sing songs. Finally, at three years of age, the child casually told its mother. We found granddad in his old workshop in the basement. When things were explained, he was happy to go into the Spirit World, knowing he could visit his grandson under much warmer circumstances.

SOLDIERS IN THE RAIN

Battlegrounds, particularly American Civil War locations are notorious for attracting earthbound spirits of soldiers and not just those who fought in the particular war that was fought there. Veterans in spirit from other wars, sometimes centuries before, who have wandered unhappily through various haunts, are drawn to the negative energy of Civil War battlegrounds. There they find others in similar plights, all drawn by the Universal Law of Attraction which does not discriminate.

While writing this book, accompanied by my partner Betty Lou and a clairvoyant Joan B. from our development circle we visited the Military Cemetery at Sackets Harbor situated at the eastern end of Lake Ontario. The area featured in the War of 1812, and while driving by the cemetery, I could often hear voices.

On this particular evening, we arrived just before dusk and made contact with the spirits living there. A sergeant who claimed to be in charge said there were seventy-two soldiers needing help. "We are all waiting for orders," he said. "It's pouring with rain. There's not much cover and it's bloody uncomfortable."

How long it had been raining for them was never explained. For us, it was a warm summer's evening with not a raindrop in sight. That's how weird these things can get when working with earthbound spirits..

The three of us agreed that seventy-two was correct. I made sure that all the group were ready to "transfer out to a better place." An affirmative response came through and we conducted a short ceremony, and within a few minutes, my guides confirmed all the men had crossed over. Using dowsing rods and pendulums we affirmed the cemetery was clear.

A month later while driving past the cemetery, there were new voices. "We will have to go back soon," I told Betty Lou. "The latent energy has attracted some newcomers."

REQUIREMENTS FOR RESCUE

Some people may ask: "Why don't the spirit guides and helpers work to rescue earthbound spirits?"

It's a good question. The problem is earthbounds become so frustrated and depressed they are totally grounded. If you have ever observed a depressed person you will know they very rarely look up, because if they did, they would not be so depressed.

The requirement for rescuing an earthbound is (1) they believe there is a better place, (2) they desire to go there (3) there are loved ones and friends waiting to welcome them. With those three in place earthbounds will voluntarily look up into the cosmic light that shines above. The moment they see that energy, they are drawn towards it. At that point it is the continuation of the regular transition into the Spirit World. It is the task of the rescuer to skillfully achieve these requirements.

CONDUCTING A SPIRIT RESCUE

The radical spiritualist bent on becoming a spirit rescuer should be totally confident in communicating with earthbound spirits, spirit guides and helpers, along with God, the Universal Mind.

He or she should be clean in thought, word and deed, in other words be morally grounded, and have unconditional love for themselves and the Universe.

He or she should know that spirit rescue is a healing that is of the highest order. Think about it. How many people are there around who are prepared to do this work, are completely clear of fears and a False Self, and want to work for the good of the Universe. Spirit rescuers are mystical warriors.

EACH RESCUE IS UNIQUE

A teacher can give advice on how to do it, but the best rescuers are those who learn from experience and each event, each rescue is a unique experience. Some are easy, some laboriously difficult, but one learns from each one.

So, here are the basics on how to do it.

Say a prayer of protection before commencing. Ask Infinite Intelligence, or whoever you pray to, to give you guidance, strength and protection.

187

Ask that your healing guide be at your side for counseling, observing and to tell you that your mission is accomplished.

Establish how many earthbound spirits are involved, a lonely isolated individual or a group of a hundred or more. Do not be surprised if a voice (or your pendulum) tells you there are a thousand. It can happen.

If there is one spirit earthbound who is clinging to a home or a particular place, get a profile from family and friends. Discover if the person had loved ones and close friends in the Spirit World. The more information the rescuer has, the easier and more effective is the talk-through and rescue.

If there is a multiplicity of earthbounds such as soldiers, the rescuer needs to determine the leader, the spirit in charge. There is always someone who will be the leader of the pack, a spokesperson. Discover if the leader is spiritual and what he or she believes about God, Heaven and any church. Find out what they know about their condition. Some are aware they are dead, some think they are in a coma, while others believe someone will give them orders and they will transfer out. Do not be surprised if everyone in the group rejects being rescued because some fears still exist among earthbounds. Ask the leader to assemble all those who wish to "go home."

Preparing for the Rescue. Be kind, considerate and compassionate, even with spirits that created their own predictament, and by this I mean people who killed themselves through deliberate life termination or reckless acts such as driving. It is not your job to judge or admonish.

It is best to describe the next world, Summerland, Heaven, the Astral World. Make it attractive.

"There is a place which is different from the Earth. There is no physical pain, discomforts, or hurts. Each one of you is a spirit and you are on a journey, a journey home where you will meet loved ones, friends and others you have known...spirits who have learned to love in the true meaning of the word.

Many loved ones who have gone ahead are waiting to help you with warm, wonderful, loving arms. They know of your plight and they are ready, able and willing to help you come home. There is no judgment for what happened, only total love for you. Because you are a good person, an intelligent person, and it's all right to be good, intelligent and be loved."

If possible from research, use names of loved ones that the earthbound spirit will recognize.

Providing an anchor. If you look near me you will see my spirit helper. (Describe your healing guide) In my rescue cases I might say: *"My helper is Chang, a very old and wise spirit who used to be a doctor in 19th century China. He has helped many souls to complete their journeys into the Spirit World, and he's here now to help us. Look, and you will see him."* Do something similar on your own guides. Earthbounds have to be told your spirit guide exists or they may not see him or her. Guides and earthbounds are on different levels until told where to look.

Raising the vibration. The task here is getting the earthbound spirits to look up, an act which raises their vibrations, and prepares for their release from the Earth plain.

"If you are ready to complete your journey, and you may already feel the spirits and energies of loved ones and friends around us, I ask that you raise your heads...and look up...look up...look up and see the beautiful white light that is shining above you. Know that you are loved...leave all your hurts and miseries behind. All that is over now. Look up and feel the beautiful white light beckoning you...this is the entrance, the gateway to your next home where you will be helped, loved and given strength and renewed energy. Look up...look up...and feel the time is now...time to complete your journey home."

The secret here is to repeat the command to "look up" which frees them from the depression of being earthbound. Do not let up with this, keep talking about loved ones waiting, a place of love and peace. It is a key requirement to raise the vibration of those who are earthbound.

SIGNS OF DEPARTURE

There will come a point when you will notice the energy is changing. The coldness that surrounds one or more earthbound starts to change, almost as if there is a warm breeze. You may well notice the area around your feet warming first and moving up through the body to the very top of your head. At this point you can stop talking, and be quiet, almost in a meditative state, waiting for the words from your guide or helper.

"*Robert,*" Chang has said on many an occasion; "*We have them. They are all safe now. Love and Light.*"

Conclude by offering a prayer of thanks to whoever you pray to, then go home and get on with your life, knowing that you have just given valuable assistance in healing the spiritual lives of those known as earthbounds.

FOR THE CRIPPLE MINDED

It's unfortunate but that are among the human community those who thrive on negativity, and they may suggest that a spirit rescue is an exorcism. No way! An exoricism is removing a negative entity that has taken possession of a sick or weak willed person. Such cases are rare and require special skills. Earthbounds never possess although they will attempt to make their situation known. Spirit rescue is a release of spirits who would have normally made a safe transition into the loving realms of the Spirit World, but somehow became snagged in the process. They do not possess anyone, but they do deserve to be rescued. Spirit rescue is a wonderful healing and they all need our help. That is one of the critical missions of the radical spiritualist..

FURTHER STUDIES

While a lot of spirit rescuers work alone or in a small group of two or three, the best place to learn spirit rescue is in a good development circle headed by an established medium. Here you will be able to see and feel a spirit rescue conducted, and learn the do's and don'ts that come with it. Ensure that your psychic energy is maintained on a high vibration through Prana exercises and that you always keep an open mind when it comes to spiritual beliefs. Once you have the demonstrated ability, be prepared to work as a spirit rescuer anytime, anyplace.

One final word: Never, ever say to an earthbound that you *"believe"* in the Afterlife. It is important to *"know"* there is an Afterlife.

A MEMO TO SPIRITUALISTS AND SPIRITUAL CENTERS

Develop a specific Spirit Rescue group whose members are trained and "on call" to anyone with symptoms of an earthbound spirit such as "coldness" in the house. Advertise its existence in the local media. There is no charge, but you can invite donations for mileage.

17

LIVING WITH
YOUR RIGHT COLOR

WHAT IS THE BEST COLOR for you physically, mentally and spiritually?

Many people are not aware of the power of colors and many go through their lives completely ignorant of the fact that they are wearing and living among the incorrect band of colors. It happened to me.

For many years as a journalist, news photographer, broadcaster and later a public relations manager I always wore different shades of brown. Come to think of it, when I was in the British Royal Air Force serving in Egypt, we wore lightweight khaki shirts and shorts. As a journalist it was brown sports jackets, brown or grey pants, and in corporate life it was brown suits. Very smart, but the wrong color.

Tom Passey pulled me aside one day when I was learning metaphysics. *"Bob, how come you always wear brown? It's not your color."* After I stared at him quizzically, he went on: *"Brown is an Earth color. It will always pull you down. You have been fighting it for a lot of years, but the color always wins."*

When I asked him what color should I wear, he pulled out his bounce rod which had the same effect as a pendulum, and went through the spectrum. *"Blue is your base color...navy, indigo, purple...any shades where there is a predominance of blue. Use all the others of the spectrum in moderation along with black and white."* Then he added: *"Forget brown."*

I followed Tom's advice and my energy changed, physically, mentally and spiritually. I found walking, jogging, climbing stairs and other physical activities much easier in my news colors. Studying and remembering metaphysics seemed better, and my psychic and spiritual abilities and consciousness improved substantially. It was as if I was seeing my world in a new light. I was suddenly conscious of color, which is fascinating because while I have been deficient in certain colors since birth, my auric sight is excellent. Psychic colors and auras appear as they should, and this is because psychic sight does not rely on the eyes.

COLORS INFLUENCE EVERYONE

Every substance on Earth contains color. Even incoming light from stars, solar systems and galaxies contains color, normally seen as white, which in itself is multi-colored.

Many color therapists and healers say that the root cause of any sickness and disease in the body can be traced back to an imbalance, a lack of a particular color in the human system. Therefore color healing is a method of restoring the correct balance.

Like many other healing modalities, color healing has its origins in our distant past. Pythagoras, who lived in the sixth century B.C.E., used colored lights in therapeutic practice and "chroma temples" or "color halls" were established throughout the Middle East and in India. Chinese healers realized the value of color healing and this was applied to garments. Colors were carefully chosen to match the elements of nature and were aligned with the principles of yin and yang. This is a practice carried out by some Chinese manufacturers to this day.

The pioneer of modern color and light therapy was Niels Finsen (1860-1904) of Iceland and Denmark who, in the late 19th century, announced the theory that sunlight had powerful healing and health qualities.

In 1903 he became the first Danish Nobel Laureate. He was awarded the Nobel Prize in Medicine and Physiology *"in recognition of his contribution to the treatment of diseases, especially lupus vulgaris (tuberculosis luposa), with concentrated light radiation, whereby he has opened a new avenue for medical science."*

Also he found that red light inhibits the formation of smallpox scars. In Copenhagen, Denmark on Tagensvej there is a Rudolf Tegner sculpture created a year after his death. It's called "Against the Light" and shows a group of nude figures gazing towards the sun. Controversial at the time, it still stands today, better understood and appreciated. Finsen's Light Institute, now the Finsen Institute is a world leading laboratory in cancer and metastasis research.

THE CALMING BLUE LIGHT

Two California psychologists, Gerrard and Hessay in 1932 scientifically proved that blue light has a calming effect and red has a stimulating power on human minds and bodies. Blues and reds are opposites in the human spectrum, and if you recall the colors of the auras, you will know that red, orange, yellow, green, blue, indigo and violet, constitute auric colors. They are also in *the* rays of the sun and are highly beneficial to the maintenance of human health and the healing of diseases.

Another color healing pioneer about the same time as Finsen was Dr. Edwin Babbitt whose classic book *The Principles of Light and Color,* published in 1896, is still available today. He wrote: *"Sunlight is the principal curative agent in nature's laboratory and where light cannot enter, disease does. Chlorosis, anaemia, leukaemia, emaciation, muscular debility, degeneration of heart and liver, dropsical effusion, softening of bones, nervous excitability, physical deformity, stunted growth and consumption are the result of excluding oneself from the beneficial effects of sunlight."*

But Babbitt, while suggesting that sunlight's role in the recovery from chronic diseases, did point out that it should be used judiciously. Sun rays can improve digestion and nutrition, improve blood and lymph circulation and increase the elimination of toxins and impurities through the skin.

COLORS BALANCE ENERGY

Color healing, sometimes called color therapy, colorology or cromothe-rapy, is an alternative medicine method. A practitioner or therapist trained in chromotherapy can use color and light to balance energy wherever a person's body might be lacking, be it physical, mental or spiritual.

Every person is under the influence of one or several colors. The colors we select for our clothes, the rooms in our home, our offices, even our cars are all selected through our higher selves. If you feel the colors around are upsetting or do not match your feelings and psyche, get a good color chart, and with a pendulum dowse out the colors that are appropriate for you in the Here and Now.

I say "Now" because sometime along the highway of life, you may find your personal colors changing. It does happen. The good thing is, you can always check with a pendulum to ascertain if your color consciousness is changing in the Here and Now. If there is a change in your colors, it means the flow of light in your inner being is changing. This occurs more in spiritually inclined people simply because most of them are progressively evolving.

UNDERSTANDING AND HEALING WITH COLOR

Let's take a look at colors and see how they can be applied in your life..

RED: People under the influence of red lead a physically active life, particularly in adolescence. It reflects heat, fire and anger. Red heals and balances muscles particularly sore muscles, treats constipation, colon, anemia and the adrenals. Red stimulates emotions, happiness and life. Red clothes on a woman stimulates male sex drive. An imbalance or lack of red brings listlessness and apathy. When used as a tonic, red will normally treat such afflictions as rheumatism, low blood pressure, cramps, paralysis, anemia and some cases of tuberculosis. Red light and red vegetables help restore this color in the body. Red people who are balanced, normally care about humanity and work to help others.

ORANGE: Because orange is a mix of red and yellow, it has many of the qualities outlined above in Red. Orange is both useful for stimulating blood supply and circulation, and it strengthens and energizes the nervous system. It is beneficial in the treatment of low self-esteem and in the treatment of digestive, liver, pancreas, gall bladder, spleen and blood sugar problems. Orange stirs intimacy, improves digestion, enhances self-approval and helps overcome shyness and some fears.

YELLOW: This is considered to be the color of wisdom among yellow-balanced people. A lack of yellow indicates jealousy, self-sabotage, lack of will power, slow learning and a tendency towards depression. Yellow works to restore oxygenation, better breathing, steadier nerves, and a better outlook on life. A person who is balanced in yellow is a well tended fire, and is normally mentally and intellectually balanced with good energy, joy and happiness.

GREEN: Comprising blue and yellow, green is regarded as a color of harmony and healing. Most healers have variations of greens in their aura. People with a balanced green are full of love and they spread love rays throughout their environment. People with prevalent greens in their system are often to be found outdoors on farms, parks and gardens. They make good teachers for young children. Green tranquilizes. Greens make good counselors—as well as healers--and their value and ability is to listen to others, and by listening, this in itself is healing. Greens love children and all animals, wild or domesticated and are generally easy going. They rarely get angry, but when they do, they are highly disturbed and hurt. Greens are perfectionists, and are rarely satisfied with their work. An imbalance of Green produces a lack of responsiveness. They leave important issues and jobs undone and will work on unimportant things. A deficiency in Green results in insomnia, thymus problems, allergies and possible high blood pressure. These people need green light to restore the nervous system, an ability to relax, which in turn reduces high blood pressure. Green vegetables help color healing.

BLUE: This color comes in all sizes. Sky Blue is sacred. It is the symbol of one-ness with God, Infinite Intelligence, the Creator. You will find Sky

Blues among many doctors, nurses, priests, physicians, some missionaries and priests, spiritual mediums and inspirational speakers. They are all cosmic-conscious servants of the Universe and Humanity. So therefore Blue is a spiritual color. It is also a sedative, great for reducing pain, curbing bleeding and the healing of burns. The deepness of Blue is relative to the level of spirituality. This color is good for blood cleansing, ear infections, nerve soreness, breathing problems and coughing. A bluish-green helps neuro transmitters, absorption of vitamins and minerals, back pain, thyroid, throat and skin conditions.

INDIGO: Or purple. The red warms the blood and the blue acts as a cooling antiseptic. It stimulates without being an irritant. The color purple stimulates the spleen and builds up the immune system. It maintains a potassium and sodium balance, very necessary if you are on a diuretic or weight loss regime. Purple also helps people control their appetites. It stimulates all glands including the lymph gland. Purple/Indigo is very comfortable for helping people sleep. Many people with purple objects and walls in their bedrooms have reported good sleeping habits. Purple is good for treating migraines, stomach disorders, diseases and infections in the bladder, urinary tracts, kidney swelling and frequent urination. Purple is a color for psychic enhancement and clairvoyance.

VIOLET: This color has special powers. Leonardo da Vinci proclaimed that you can increase the power of meditation ten-fold by meditating under the gentle rays of Violet, as found in Church windows. In pagan temples sections of violet stained glass were positioned to induce healing for sick people. This color inspires beauty, creativity and inspiration. It is the highest of the spiritual colors and is humanity's connection to the Cosmos, the Overself and brings spiritual guidance, wisdom and inner strength especially for those in the arts and inspirational writing. People who live in the violet light often take time out to meditate in solitude and listen to the Shabd, the Audible Sound Stream, the Voice of God. It is the light that gently surrounds and envelops the spirit as it departs for home from the body and makes its transition into the Spirit World.

WHITE: White is the perfect color; for it is all colors in perfect balance and harmony. It is light from the sun, the color of the awakened Spirit; the light of perfection; the light of the Christ and Buddha consciousness. It is also the Divine Light. Just about everyone has heard of surrounding people with the "White Light of Healing and Protection." Directing white into the aura helps stimulate the person's own divine nature into healing the Self.

HOW TO USE THE COLORS

Color healing is as simple as walking out into the sunshine on a beautiful day and spending fifteen to twenty minutes simply walking, perhaps in a park or across a meadow. The white light of the sun contains all the colors we have mentioned. If you are sensitive to ultra violet or have a sensitive skin, reduce the outdoor walking to a minimum. Your pendulum, responding through your higher self will tell you the optimal time for your exposure Now.

HELP ON THE COLOR HEALING PATH

Some sound healers I have known, have simply had incandescent lamps in metal boxes equipped with slots for holding colored filters. Some color healers venture out to filter dealers and inspect each item as if they are buying a million-dollar diamond. Filters also come in stained glass. Here again, it is best to know the colors you want before venturing out, and don't forget to take your pendulum. It will tell you whether the colored filter is the one you are seeking. There are some lamps and lenses sets already made for the aspiring color healer.

In addition there are courses offered by various organizations and some of them carry certifications which are always useful if you wish to adopt color healing as a modality in your therapy office.

Color healing is one of those modalities that the Radical Spiritualist Healer could adopt as a workable and attractive healing therapy.

At the back of this book, there is a list of sources for color healing and other modalities mentioned in this book. They are there for your information. It's up to you to find out whether they are appropriate for your use. If in doubt, use your pendulum.

Here is a thought: Your higher self, your true self can see many more colors than you can with your naked eye.

18

IN THE BEGINNING
WAS THE SHABD

IF YOU WISH TO STAY HEALTHY, have abundant energy, and do things that people half your age do not even bother to talk about, keep you body greased with Prana, that magical energy that causes things to grow, envigorates, sustains and heals.

We dealt with it in the chapter on Complete Breathing.

Prana comes from the ancient Sanscrit term meaning "Absolute Energy" or "Vital Force." It can be found in all forms of life from the smallest amoeba to human beings. It extends through all plant life to the highest form of animal life. As the Yogis say, Prana is all pervading.

As I said earlier, Prana comes from the ancient Sanscrit term meaning "Absolute Energy," or Vital Force," and every cell in your body, every atom, every molecule is energized by Prana. It is the food of the Cosmic system, and in healing it is vital to know and appreciate its qualities.

But there is another energy that swims above and through Prana, and every quester, every healer should be aware of it. Its name is Shabd. Some people call it the Audible Life Stream, Sacred Sound, and some call it the Word or the voice of God. Simply put, it is God, the Universal Mind, the Creator, Infinite Intelligence. In Theological terms it is the Word or Logos, the Divine Word as the Greek Neoplatonic teachers taught it. It is the Force and as Jesus said *"God is spirit."*

Let's try and put a handle on this. We who walk the Planet Earth are an incredibly designed bundle of muscles, bones, organs, and glands all made up of billions of cells, all vibrating in their own time and space. They are all connected and communicate back and forth with pranic energy coordinated by spirit. The spirit is you. You are spirit occupying a neat little divinely created robotic thing called the human body.

THE UNIVERSE IS A LIVING THING

Your spirit which is also called the Overself, the True Self, the Higher Self, etc., is connected constantly to the Audible Life Stream. We know that prana is the empowering energy, the gasoline, the electricity that moves and motivates us. But the Audible Life Stream is the Force with the super cosmic intelligence that not only keeps us alive and creative, it is the Force that is continually creating our World, the Solar System, our Universe and everything beyond. The Universe is a living entity, a spirit and it is alive, and we hope, well.

This brings meaning to the first chapter of the Gospel of John: *"In the beginning was the Word and the Word was with God and the Word was God. All things were made by him and without him was not anything made that was made."*

Words are sounds. Sounds can be words, as we know them, but sound can also heal as we discussed earlier in sound healing, by restoring the vibrations of cells within the human body. Dr. Jenny showed in Cymatics that if vibrations created distinct patterns in sand and other particles, then sound vibrations could also affect the human body.

Sound is powerful. It can heal and it can destroy. Recall those words from the Joshua. *"When ye hear the sound of the trumpets all the people shall shout with a great shout; and the wall of the city shall fall down flat."* Whether it occurred or not, the writer knew the power of sound, otherwise it would not have been written. Fact or fiction, it contains a major element of truth.

THE TRUTH EMERGES

Again, there is an element of truth in the Gospel of John when he wrote those very significant lines "and the Word was God."

Not too many people understand those first few verses in the Gospel of John, but it does indicate something that the ascended masters and others believe and teach. It's called the Audible Life Stream which is also known as the Sound Current, a title derived from the Hindu Shabd, meaning sound.

SOUND THROUGH INFINITE SPACE

As we discovered in the human abilities to make sound and heal people through toning, when humans speak they trigger atmospheric vibrations which can heal, restore the body to its former optimal state. However, when God speaks, the Shabd not only vibrates on an etheric level, the sound vibrates through infinite space, the Universe, the Cosmos and everything.

"God is not static, latent. He is superlatively dynamic." Those words come from philosopher Julian P. Johnson in his classic book *The Path of the Masters.* He advocates that to hear the Shabd, one needs to be trained. *"It is in fact the only way in which the Supreme One can be seen and heard—this mighty, luminous and music wave, creating and enchanting."*

As in all things spiritual and metaphysical it is always advisable for the dedicated student to find a guru or teacher who is accomplished in teaching the higher levels of learning and healing.

THE NEED TO UNDERSTAND

However it does help if one understands the human connection with God, the Universal Mind and vice versa.

The Shabd or the Sound Current is the phenomenon that Jesus, the Galilean teacher and healer refers to, and is mentioned in the Gospel of John.

Jesus says: *"You should not be surprised at my saying, You must be born again. The wind blows wherever it pleases. You hear its sound, but you cannot tell where it comes from or where it is going. So it is with everyone born of the Spirit."* (John 3:7 KJV)

Fascinating words. *"The wind blows...you hear its sound."* The teacher is giving instructions here on contacting the Current and actually hearing it.

"You must be born again," refers to the removal of the human ego, the False Self, the devil within. The False Self will attempt to block any plan to demolish or crucify its existence, and block the opportunity to be "born again" without the chains of the False Ego. If this seems extreme, go back to Chapter Five and browse over *"Escape to a New Life."*

The Audible Life Stream is heard again when the followers of Jesus were gathered to expect the Holy Spirit. It's written in Acts: *"And suddenly there came a sound from heaven, as of a rushing mighty wind, and it filled the whole house where they were sitting."* (Acts 2:2) Again it is described as a wind.

John, the writer of the last book of the New Testament knew full well of the Audible Sound Stream when he wrote: *"And I heard a voice from heaven, as the voice of many waters, and as the voice of a great thunder: and I heard the voice of harpers harping with their harps:"* (Revelation 14:2 KJB)

The Sufis, the mystics of Islam, call the Shabd, Saute Surmadi otherwise known as Abstract Sound. They say all space is filled with it.

In his book *The Mysticism of Sound and Music,* Hazrat Inayat Khan says it was the Saute Surmadi that Mohammed heard in the cave of Gar-e-Hira. Moses also heard the same sound on Mount Sinai. Jesus heard it when his Heavenly Father manifested to him in the Wilderness. Shiva, one of the members of the Hindu Trinity heard the same sounds during his deep meditative Samadhi in a cave in the Himalayas. The flute of Krishna, the Hindu deity is symbolic of the same sound. According to Hazrat Inayat, when the abstract sound is audible, all other sounds become indistinct to the mystical ear. People do not generally hear the sound because their consciousness is centered on material existence.

THE HEALING POWER OF SACRED SOUNDS

According to Hazrat Inayat those who have the ability to hear the Saute Surmadi and meditate on it, receive a variety of healing at the physical and mental levels. These include worry, anxiety, sorrow, fears and diseases. The soul is freed from captivity in the physical body. In other words the Sufi is perhaps suggesting that the False Self, the ego is defeated and the soul, the true self blooms. He says the soul of the listener becomes the all-pervading consciousness.

ATTUNING TO THE SACRED SOUND

There are various ways one can train oneself to hear the sacred sound such as sitting in solitude on the sea-shore, on the river bank or away in the hills and dales.

Some accomplish it by sitting in mountain caves, or while wandering constantly through forests and deserts, in other words avoiding material existence and influences.. Yogis and ascetics blow a horn called a Singhi or a shell known as a Shankha which awakens in them the sacred sound. Dervishes are said to play a double flute for the same purpose.

Some Native American Indians play pentatonic flutes, that is a flute with five holes and there are some marvelous creations for meditative listening. The secret is to create your own music. You really do not need to know anything about music to play and benefit from Native Indian flutes.

As we mentioned earlier, there are some great traditional Indian flautists. One is Odell Borg who says the *"Native American flute is a magical and a wonderful way to express emotions and feelings. It is very low tech yet has the most soothing, peaceful voice through which we can easily express ourselves."*

Betty Lou and I have several Native Indian flutes, and when I sit and create random notes, it happens that after a while the tones or music seem to take on a life of their own. When I asked the guides if they have anything to do with my playing, they simply laugh and say "Not us." Which leaves the question: Who or what motivates the sounds? I sometimes feel that the flute wants to play on its own. I suddenly realize I am in a deep altered state of consciousness.

Some sources say that the Shabd, the Sacred Sound is indescribable. However, the Sufi writer, Hazrat Inayat claims the sounds can be like thunder, the roaring of the sea, the jingling of bells, running water, the buzzing of bees, the twittering of sparrows, the Vina, the whistle, or the sound of the Shankha, until it finally becomes the HU.

The Healing Paths of the Radical Spiritualist have finally reached the Sacred Sound of God, the Universal Mind, the Creator and the Word of God that Heals. In two letters, HU.

THE POWER OF HU

According to Sufi philosophers and many other teachers around the world, HU is the most sacred of all sounds.

It is the beginning and end of all sounds. The beginning and end of sounds such as waves on a seashore, the whisper of a steam-engine starting, the cry of birds and animals, the echo of bells and drums, and the voices of human beings.

Listen as you or someone else starts to speak, there is that intake of breath, and again when you stop talking, there is that gentle letting go of breath. It is the softest of all sounds is the sacred HU and it is all around us and within.

God, the Creator, the Supreme Being, the Universal Mind, Infinite Intelligence has been called various names in a variety of languages, but mystics have long known that Being as Hu.

It is not a creation of men and women who walk the Earth, it simply is. It exists. It is the spirit of all sounds, all words, and it is mostly hidden throughout them all, much like the spirit that occupies a body. HU belongs to and exists in all languages. Every activity of life expresses this sound quite distinctly. The first sounds of a new born baby, the part before the first cry, is HU.

It gives a fascinating insight into the meaning of the Gospel of John: "In the beginning was the Word, and the Word was with God, and the Word was God."

Old tradition has it that Zoroaster was born of a huma tree. In this word -- hu -- represents spirit, and the rest of the word – ma'a – means water in Arabic. This could explain the deeper meaning of Jesus' message when he said: *"Except a man be born of water and of the Spirit, he cannot enter into the kingdom of God."* (KJB John 3:5)

THE MEANING OF WATER

There was the occasion when Jesus met a woman of Samaria at Jacob's Well, and during the exchange Jesus the teacher and healer made the statement: *"Whoever drinks of this water shall thirst again, but whoever drinks of the water I shall give him shall never thirst."* (KJB John 4).

The Gospel of John makes a wonderful study for all students of metaphysics and the teachings of Jesus. It is his encounter with the woman in which he demonstrates his clairvoyant powers.

So Hazrat Inayat Khan and many other mystics teach that the word *"Human"* means a God-conscious being, God-realized, or the God-person. It is interesting to note that words found in the Bible such as Eloi, Elohim and Alleluya, are all corruptions of the original word Allah-Hu.

WORKING WITH THE AUDIBLE LIFE STREAM

Dr. Julian Johnson in his classic book *The Path of the Masters* describes the Path as the Royal Highway of the Saints, the El Camino Real. *"It is the medicine which cures every sickness. It is the one remedy which the great physician, the Master, offers for the relief of all ills."*

A succession of great teachers including many saints have offered this Path, this Fountain of Life, as the only actual means of spiritual liberation.

Lao-tze, considered the greatest of the pre-Confucian philosophers and who lived about 604 to 521 BCE is the founder of the Tao otherwise known as *The Way*. The most important text in Taoist philosophy is *Tao-Te-Ching* otherwise known as the *Book of the Way and of Virtue*. Various scholars claim the text existed long before Lao-tze, and some academics question whether the Chinese philosopher even existed at all, mainly because he disappeared.

Will Durant in the first volume of *The Story of Civilization: Our Oriental Heritage* describes the Tao, meaning the Way, as a Way of Nature, a way of wise living and quite literally a road.

It is a way of refusing to think because the Taoist considers thinking a superficial affair, an excuse only for argument and more harmful than beneficial to life.

In other words, intellectuality will not get a spiritual quester to the higher levels of God-consciousness, and it will not get you into the Way of the Shabd, the Audible Life Stream.

THE VALUE OF MODESTY

The Taoist bent on living within the flow of the Sacred Sound leads a modest life with quiet contemplation of nature.

The teachings of Lao-tze who lived five centuries before Jesus, possessed similar messages, and these are listed in H.A. Giles' 1901 book *The History of Chinese Literature*: "*If you do not quarrel, no one on earth will be able to quarrel with you...Recompense injury with kindness...To those who are good, I am good, and to those who are not good I am also good. There's more: To those who are sincere I am sincere, and to those who are not sincere I am also sincere...The softest thing in the world dashes and overcomes the hardest...There is nothing in the world softer or weaker than water, and yet for attacking things that are firm and strong there is nothing that can take precedence of it.*"

Compare these Taoisms to the teachings of Jesus contained in the Sermon on the Mount and you will find they mirror each other. Both are instructions for a higher life, both call for people to devote their lives to the Tao, the Way, the Sacred Sound, the Shabd, the Audible Life Stream.

Recall the quote of Jesus we used earlier in this chapter on being born again: "*The wind blows wherever it pleases. You hear its sound, but you cannot tell where it comes from or where it is going. So it is with everyone born of the Spirit.*"

THE HEAVENLY SOUNDS IN SPIRIT

There are times when one can hear the Shabd or the Audible Life Stream. The problem is it is generally indescribable and you may think your making it up, or you have "sounds" in your ears.

People who have done a lot of astral projection work pass through the stream and will report a rushing sound or a wind, even a hissing sound as they go. Robert Monroe reports on this in *Journeys Out of the Body*. It is the same with people going through Near-Death experiences, many fail to recognize it as Sacred Sound.

Most people who have died and crossed over into the Spirit World experience the welcoming sounds of the Shabd even though they might not have had metaphysical and spiritual leanings while in the physical.

The Sacred Sound is quite evident in the Spirit World. Robert Hugh Benson, the British clergyman who crossed over into Spirit in 1914 and who dictated his book *Life in the World Unseen* to author Anthony Borgia noted this phenomenon.

Benson said through the vast galaxy of colors in the spirit world their ears are *"being constantly assailed with the sounds of music; that we are living, in fact, in an eternity of music that is sounding and resounding without remission."* He added that folk in Spirit please themselves, whether they wish to listen to it or not. *"The secret is personal attunement."*

NO TWO HEAR IT ALIKE

My spirit companion Paul says the Shabd or the Audible Life Stream is nothing like Earth music created by the classical composers or even the jazz musicians. *"It is not structured musically as you would know it, and no two people or spirits hear it alike. It affects different listeners in different ways. It's quite confusing to some musicians who come over. However, if you attune to it, your life in our world is enhanced and your progression moves accordingly."*

What value is it for people on Earth? I posed the obvious question.

"Sacred Sound is abundant with blessings—if you allow it," said Paul. *"Problem is, one has to believe in it, adopt it, and allow healing to happen. You recall Jesus said his Father would send his disciples the Holy Spirit? Well, that's another name for the Audible Sound Current. People make a lot of fuss over the fact they were able to speak in various languages—*

that's simple. When the Disciples heard the Sacred Sound they were blessed with vibrant health, mentally and physically. They were imbued with their teachings that had been curtailed by the removal of their teacher, Jesus. They were able to conduct healings, understand ancient spiritual philosophies that benefit all humankind, and speak on them. The Holy Spirit is available to all. You simply need to clear your mind, be quiet and listen."

EXERCISE: TUNING TO THE SHABD. Find yourself a quiet place where you will not be disturbed and all is totally quiet. Sit in a straight, comfortable chair, or if you can, kneel, or better still adopt the Lotus position.

Spend a few minutes performing the Yogi Complete Breath, then with eyes closed, create a ball of the purest white light you can imagine above your head. Bring it down so it creates an imaginary cocoon of energy.

Allow your consciousness to feel the peace within. Then, taking a good, deep breath, with lips barely open like in a kissing shape, allow the sacred word Hu to flow gently through your lips, just like what it is, a mantra. It will be a soft, flowing whoooooo, and if anyone is standing near you, they will think it is a low whispered hum. You may, if you wish, perform the Hu meditation as an internal chant.

Do this for ten or fifteen minutes. Then sit in silence and observe how you feel. Then thank whoever you pray to, rise and get on with your life.

Remember, this is a Sacred Sound. Do this exercise daily, and be advised to keep a small notebook, journaling your feelings and any experiences that may occur. As noted at the beginning, you may well discover a number of health benefits. Note them in your journal. Do not expect benefits, allow them to come.

One final word, resist the temptation to imagine what the Audible Life Stream, the Shabd looks, feels or sounds like. If you have an image of God, let it go. This could be the old False Self resorting to memory.

Oh, yes. Whatever you do, love yourself for doing it. This is your spiritual insurance and it pays great dividends.

19

SHARING THE LIGHT
BEYOND THE VEIL

THROUGHOUT OUR JOURNEY to discover the Healing Paths of the Radical Spiritualist, there is one Path we really have not explored or considered and that is maintaining optimum health. So many people only start being concerned with their health when the doctor says: *"You have a problem."* Then it is panic stations.

There are all sorts of gurus and trainers out there who are offering services to the 60 million Baby Boomers and those who are "getting on a bit." They do everything from helping with financial needs and resources, housing and lifestyle, travel, relationships, community involvement, nutrition and physical health.

They talk about everything except death. It's the bogey word. So we come up with such expressions as crossing over, meeting his maker, gone to Boot Hill, she's at the end of the road, the final curtain, kicking the bucket. No one likes to mention the D word, unless of course you are a Spiritualist, and the Spiritualist will retort: *"There's no such thing as death."*

Spiritualists see life and death quite differently.

"Life here and life hereafter is all one life whose continuity of consciousness is unbroken by that mere change in form whose process we call death," said Lilian Whiting, American journalist and author who was one of the first women newspaper editors. Ms Whiting is quoted in the Spiritualist Manual of the National Spiritualist Association of Churches in the United States.

Poets and writers through the ages have frequently talked about death. John Milton, the 17th century English poet, wrote: *"Death is the golden key that opens the palace of eternity."* Sir Rabindranath Tagore, India's poet, philosopher, composer and Nobel Prize winner put it this way: *"Death: where the changing mist of doubts will vanish at a breath, and the mountain peaks of eternal truth will appear."*

In spite of the colorful, dramatic prose of the poets, most people are unable to accept either the death of a loved one, or the fact that sooner or later, death will come upon them.

DEATH IS INEVITABLE

Death is a subject which is evaded, ignored, and denied by our youth-worshipping, material-oriented society because the fear of death is the prototype of human anxiety. As Elisabeth Kübler-Ross, author of the ground-breaking 1969 book *On Death and Dying* pointed out: "It is almost as if we have taken on death as just another disease to be conquered. But the fact is death is inevitable."

In western society, death is the great bogey. It is the phobia that fuels many other phobias. Fundamental Christians traditionally talk of the dreaded Last Judgment, an event pointedly mentioned in both the Apostolic and Nicene Creeds, and chanted by many church-goers every Sunday. The image here is that sinners -- and everyone according to the doctrines -- are sinners, will be consigned to the horrors of Purgatory or the everlasting agonies of Hell.

If that concept is fading, a more popular fear is emerging that death takes us into everlasting nothingness--that you stay buried in the grave forever until Judgment Day. Reading the Old Testament compounds the fears. "For dust thou art, and unto dust thou shalt return." (Genesis 3:19). To cap it all, the Roman Catholic Church puts the squeeze on its flock by saying it's a mortal sin not to come to church on Sundays.

It is little wonder that so many people, particularly the older folk are terrified about dying. *"Some people are so afraid to die that they never begin to live."* These were words from Henry Jackson Van Dyke, the American Presbyterian clergyman and author, who lived in the 19th century at a time when Modern Spiritualism was starting to flourish and changing our concept of death.

The way the Spiritualists put it: The only death that does occur, is the death or the ceasing to function of the physical body. It's like the spirit taking off an overcoat and leaving it behind to be buried in an expensive casket and mourned by a whole lot of loved ones who feel sorry because there's a gap, a space where the body used to be. The spirit that occupied that body lives on and is welcomed joyously by loved ones and relatives in the Spirit World.

DEATH IS AN ILLUSION

Strictly speaking, there is no such thing as death. It's a lie, a phrase used by well-intended but ignorant people. As the great Indian Mystic, Yogi Ramacharaka, said: *"Death is an illusion growing from ignorance. There is no death--there is nothing but Life. Life does not cease for even a single instant--life persists while Nature makes her changes."*

These words summarize death and the philosophy of Modern Spiritualism: *"We affirm that the existence and personal identity of the individual continues after the change called death."*

Since the veil between the two worlds was split in 1848 at Hydesville, New York, thousands upon thousands of people the world over have received greetings and meaningful messages from departed love-ones and others, and this has been scientifically and personally confirmed. Fears of death are slowly being eroded and the light of eternal grace is being confirmed. But old habits, particularly religious habits die hard.

BELIEF IN LIFE AFTER DEATH

The American Association of Retired Persons -- AARP -- in its September 2007 edition, had Bill Newcott reporting on a survey of people over 50: He wrote: *"... we found that people 50 and over tend to be downright conventional in their basic beliefs: nearly three quarters (73 percent) agree with the statement 'I believe in life after death.' Women are a lot more likely to believe in an afterlife (80 percent) than men (64 percent)."* (www.aarpmagazine.org)

Sir Walter Scott, the great Scottish poet and novelist, put it this way: *"Is death the final sleep? No it is the last and final awakening."*

Still, while people are still buzzing around enjoying life, the final dawning of an encounter with death does provoke uncertainty, a fear of loss of control and stress.

THE SON 'TERRIFIED OF DYING"

Knowing that loved ones are waiting on the Other Side is a concept hard to believe. Some years ago, a mother called me: "My son is terminally ill in the Vancouver Cancer Control Clinic. He's terrified of dying. He doesn't believe in anything, and he's very depressed."

Ted was in his mid-thirties, married with two very young children. I had recently heard Elisabeth Kübler-Ross talking on the five stages of dying - denial, rage and anger, bargaining with God, depression, and acceptance. Ted's bargaining with God was a disaster. "I don't believe in God or the so-called hereafter," he said, and he was now totally depressed.

No one ever dies alone, and this was true for Ted. His hospital room was bounding with spirits, except for the fact he could not see them. One very dominant woman in spirit stood on the other side of the bed. A rosy-red hefty face, her sleeves rolled up above the elbows, she said: "Tell Ted to get crackin'."

I relayed the message, and described the woman in spirit as appearing like the traditional Irish Washerwoman. Ted's eyes regarded me suspiciously. "Sounds like granny. She lived in Nova Scotia. I lived with her as a kid."

"On your seventh birthday you caught your arm in my mangle," said Granny. "And that was a to-do."

"That's Granny!" Suddenly, Ted was more than interested. I described some of the spirits manifesting in the room, and he quickly recognized departed relatives and an old school pal killed in an auto accident.

Ted was convinced, but suddenly developed a great thirst for knowledge. I spent two afternoons afternoon talking to Ted about the World of

214

Spirit, the Other Side, and how this all coincided with the ancient teachings. *"It makes so much sense,"* he said, tears flowing down his pale face. *"Why didn't someone tell me all this before?"* I didn't answer.

The changing mist of doubts had vanished at a breath, and the mountain peaks of eternal truth had started to appear. He was now in the Kübler-Ross Acceptance stage at peace with himself and his family. Five days later he passed over. And Granny, the Irish Washerwoman, was waiting along with the others to assist with his transition.

THE CAUSE OF FEAR IS IGNORANCE

Considering that death exempts no one, it is important that we are able to face death wisely. The leading cause of fear is ignorance and fear of the unknown. Other major factors are: attachment, or the fear of losing people and possessions; lack of preparation by loved ones who may be dependent upon the dying person; and unexpressed emotions and feelings, and feeling guilty for unresolved situations. These are the basic points traditional counselors recognize. .

But Modern Spiritualists are able to go further. They point to scientific research carried out by Dr. Raymond Moody. He authored the classic book *Life After Life, The Investigation of a Phenomenon-Survival of Bodily Death* on common experiences of people who have undergone clinical death and lived again. In a survey on near-death experiences Dr. Moody found that all of the participants experienced God's unconditional love. Dr. Elisabeth Kübler-Ross wrote the foreword in the book.

In near-death experience, people see themselves separate from the physical body, and view what is happening around them. Their descriptions of what they saw and heard are often quite easily validated, in spite of the fact they were clinically dead. In addition to this, mediums are able to convey accurate and meaningful messages from departed loved ones.

Spiritualism when rationally explained removes all fear of death. It opens the windows of the spirit world, and the light floods in. It teaches that death is not the cessation of life, but mere change of condition. It teaches that there is no dreaded judgment day, but that man, through what he sows, creates his own negative or positive living.

SPIRITUALISM TEACHES HOW TO LIVE

In essence, Modern Spiritualism teaches people not only how to die but how to live. This was aptly expressed by Michel Eyquem de Montaigne, the 16th century French essayist, "He who should teach men to die, would, at the same time, teach them to live."

This is a great healing opportunity for Spiritualists who can provide invaluable help for families with loved ones about to make their transition into the Spirit World. A few of them already do, but the ability to help is low key, generally unpublicized, and happens through personal referrals.

A DEATH IN ST. AUSTELL, ENGLAND

In 1979 in the days before her body quit under spinal cancer and she crossed into the Spirit World, my mother was in the Mount Edgcumbe Hospice in St. Austell, England. I flew from Canada to see her. I knew little about metaphysics, little about the Afterlife, and less about healing. I spent several days with her at her apartment in the Cornish town. It was grueling to see her trying to get up, but her spine had failed her and the doctor had given her a few days to live. I was immersed in a frustrated anger and very bitter. Frustrated, I knew that spirits existed because my father had come through on the day he died a couple of years before. But as she was approaching the end of her life I didn't know enough about the Afterlife to put my mother's mind at ease.

Mum told me she had long ago left the Anglican Church to join the Methodists. There, she had found good friends, but somehow had not clicked with God or "any of His angels," she said as we sat quietly.

MESSAGE OF HOPE

Years later, she came through in spirit. I apologized for not being able to explain the process of crossing over into Spirit so as to ease her mind.

"Two things," she said. *"One, I was not alone on that day. Dad was back, so was my sister Eydie and others. They put my mind at ease. I still*

didn't know where I was going and that bothered me." She paused and gazed straight at me: "You know now about death and the transition to our world, and your spirit helpers are very good. You have the opportunity to help the ones who fear the final days on Earth. Put their minds at ease. Go Bobbie. Spread the word. Write the message of hope."

Close family members, loved ones who are already in Spirit, will often appear in the hospital rooms and bedrooms of those close to departure. Much like Ted's grandmother did. Much like my mother's loved ones in Spirit did. People about to die are surrounded by loved ones in Spirit several days in advance of the transition. No one ever dies alone and hospital patients often see and recognize loved ones at various times prior to their transition.

SOMETHING NOT TO SAY

When a dying person tells visitors, *"Dad was here this morning. He sat and held my hand."* The worst thing for the stolid linear-minded family member to say is: *"You were just imagining it, mom. He's been gone ten years."* That is a form of spiritual abuse. Chances are Dad was there, plus a lot of other loved ones and relatives.

If person who is expected to die in the near future and insists on clinging to life, a Spiritualist can provide loving assistance. It is a great opportunity for all concerned. The medium can relay messages from spirits in the room, trying wherever possible to validate their existence.

"They are all here, your loved ones and friends, waiting to help you cross over safely into their world."

If the Spiritualist has knowledge of the Spirit World, he or she can talk to the patient, and describe the love and compassion that exists there, and the new life. The Spiritualist should always be warm and caring, but always maintain a firm voice demonstrating knowledge. If the Spiritualist is short on information about life in the Spirit World, he or she should get educated, read books dictated by spirits, or spend some time talking to his or her own spirit guides. That's what they are there for: to educate.

A basic dialogue I use for anyone waiting to die is as follows: *"Your loved ones in the Spirit World (or Heaven) are waiting for you, and they are surrounding you with all their love. There will come a time soon when you will feel a light, a beautiful golden white light above your head. When you see or feel that light you will know it is time to go. Simply close your eyes and allow God's angels and your loved ones to lift you up. You will probably hear some beautiful music, that's the sounds of the Holy Spirit, God's voice calling you home, and that's all right. It is your time. You have our blessings. Go with God."*

Please feel free to modify and improve the above and use it whenever you have the opportunity to help a soul cross over into the Summerland or Spirit World.

WORK TO THE SPIRITUAL LEVEL

Sometimes a son or daughter will ask you to help in the transition. Families collectively are hesitant to do anything that will accelerate an aged or sick person to die in comfort and peace. If the dying person is alone and appears to have no relatives, and still clings to life, ask the doctor in charge if it's all right to give "counseling" or a "dying blessing." They will normally agree.

Incidentally, always start and conclude with a prayer, and always work to the spiritual level of the person your helping with their transition.

If, as the reader of this book, you are still clinging to the "resurrection of the body" teachings in the Creed and various other dogmas, refer to Halley's Bible Handbook, written for students of the Christian Bible. It states: *"Death is merely an incident in passing from one phase of existence to another."* Trained Spirit communicators – mediums -- prove this daily and it is high time, they seized the opportunity of publicly offering to help people drawing their curtains on their earthly lives with the message of hope: *"There is Light Beyond the Veil and we can share it with you."*

THE HEALING GIFT OF LOVE

This is an exercise in using your Mind and the healing power of love. It comes in two parts and anyone can do it, the second part will produce a love-loaded message for a loved one or friend in hospital or a hospice.

The First Part: Developing the Power. Find a tray and obtain half a dozen clean or better still, polished stones or marbles. Place them all in the tray. Now, select one that is different. Hold it in your hand and talk to it. Tell it that you love it and are surrounding it with all the love in your heart. Do this two or three times. Then place it back on the tray. Close your eyes and shuffle the stones. Then, holding the palm of your hand facing downward, about two inches above the stones, move it horizontally. When you come to the "loving" stone, your hand should feel warm. Pick up the stone. You may have to do this two or three times. Most people do it the first time.

Recognize that you have sent love energy to an object and it is radiating that love.

The Second Part: Sending the Gift of Healing. When you have a loved one or a friend who needs healing or is waiting to cross over into the Spirit World, obtain an item that is meaningful, perhaps a small doll, a teddy bear, a pillow, a small blanket or some fluffy object that they can hold.

Relax and spend a few minutes holding the object. Tell it how much you love it. Surround it with all the love in your heart. Do this several times over a day or two. Then place it in a bag and take it to your sick friend. They will feel and benefit from your loving energy. If the person is about to die, they will much appreciate your gift because they will not only feel your love in the item, but your presence too.

20

THE COMPASSIONATE HEALER

WHAT QUALITIES, what philosophy, what energy must the radical spiritualist possess to be an effective healer?

If you put this question to a forum you may be surprised by the answers. Some will suggest empathy, sympathy, love of the sick, benevolence, kindness, love of god, rightfulness, ethical, duty, goodness, honor Jesus, and pity. Some will suggest all of these.

A recent client, we'll call her Thelma, came for spiritual guidance. *"Every time I attempt to send absent healing to the poor hurting people of Haiti, I burst into a flood of tears. I cannot help pitying them."*

"Why do you pity them?"

Surprised, she peered through teary eyes. *"Is there another way?"*

"What does pity do? Does it help the people of Haiti?"

She became pensive. *"I suppose not, but I've always been told to pity people who are hurt. My mother always..."*

"Well, you will not be an effective healer by crying and pitying people," I said. *"Unfortunately you and a whole lot of other people across the world have been taught to help people by pitying them. "* I did not tell her it was another aspect of the conditioned mind, the False Self working.

In the world of healing, pity is a useless and sometimes dangerous word. When people send pity, they generate thought-energy loaded with feelings that do not help in any way other than to say "Our unhappy, grief-stricken thoughts are with you." People suffering from a catastrophic disaster need to receive divine love, unconditional love, a love that inspires healing and strength. Healers who channel the healing spirit of

God, should simply send it as a prayer form or absent healing. The whole thing should be a positive action performed without any sentimental displays, such as pity.

"Let's stop identifying with the hurts people suffer, otherwise you will go on weeping. Let us identify with healing and the power of healing. Why do you want to heal?"

"Because I wish to heal others. I love healing."

"If there was a man accused of mass murders lying on the sidewalk and he was dying from bullet wounds, would you give him healing?"

Thelma pondered the question, then shuddered. "I feel awful. I don't think I could. He's bad man and bad men do not deserve healing."

One of the downfalls in healing is a tendency to judge. Thelma, still in the clutches of the False Self, the negative ego, judged the victims of the Haiti earthquake through the "face" of pity. She then subconsciously judged the man accused of mass murder and would not have given him healing.

Rumi, the 13th century Sufi mystic wrote: *"Your task is not to seek for love, but merely to seek and find all the barriers within yourself that you have built against it."* If we have blocks preventing us from administering healing we need to seek, find and dissolve them, because they are faces of the False Self.

The Radical Spiritualist on the true healing path does not judge, does not pick and choose who or not to heal. They simply offer themselves as instruments for healing to all living things. The true healer is beyond the limitations of beliefs, free from the faces of the False Self, free from the boundaries of time, free from social judgments. The true healer is the epitome of compassion.

SO WHAT IS COMPASSION?

Let us take a look at what it is not. J. Krishnamurti said that *"Thought cannot, by any means whatsoever, cultivate compassion."* Likewise, you cannot *"think"* yourself to love anything or anybody. If you have to think yourself into a compassionate state, you fail to understand true healing and the whole significance of life.

If you resort to "thought" to do something, fall in love, be a patriot for your country, or be a compassionate healer, you are still in the grip of the mechanical mind, the False Self which is living on old memories of things you "should do." Compassion is not sentiment, wooly sympathy or empathy, or something cultivated by being kind, polite, gentle and a whole lot of other *"nice"* things. "Compassion comes into being only when thought has come to an end at its very root," said Krishnamurti.

Other philosophers have spoken on compassion.

Dr. Arthur Jersild, a teacher and expert in Child Psychology said: *"It is through compassion that a person achieves the highest peak and deepest reach in his or her search for self-fulfillment."*

Matthew Fox, an Episcopal priest and a popular mystical author, who was expelled from the Dominican Order said: *"Compassion is not a moral commandment but a flow and overflow of the fullest human and divine energies."*

Then there was Thomas Merton, the Trappist monk and poet, author and social activist who wrote: *"Compassion is the keen awareness of the interdependence of all things."*

THE HUMAN CONNECTION

As you may well have perceived, it is easier to say what compassion is not, than what it is. Yes, it is a "search for self-fulfillment," and yes it is "a flow and overflow of the fullest human and divine energies," and yes, it is the "keen awareness of the interdependence of all things."

Once upon a time, in the early 1950s, I recall reading a short science fiction story by Ray Bradbury *A Sound of Thunder.* Set in 2055, a hunter named "Eckels" goes on the adventure of a lifetime, venturing back in time to hunt for a Tyrannosaurus Rex. He and other hunters are warned to stay on the paths. It was explained the necessity of minimizing the effects on the ancient environment could snowball into catastrophic changes in history. Well, Eckels gets mud on his boots from leaving the path. The safari returns to Earth to find the English language has changed, people and buildings are different and a fascist candidate has won the presidential elections. What happened back in time? Eckels' boot crushed a butterfly.

Almost sixty years ago the story was intriguing but to a young mind, my own, it was to dawn on me years later the true significance of that fine story story.

I was reminded of Eckels and the Butterfly when we watched the BBC's excellent production of *Planet Earth* which has fifteen 50-minute episodes. The dramatic message really comes over that life is a coexistent format. Whether we like it or not, we are interdependent. Plants, animals and humans rely on each other to survive. Each provides something that the other needs. In most cases it is food.

NO MAN IS AN ISLAND

For instance Krill is a shrimp-like marine invertebrate that lives near the bottom of the food chain. It relies on phytoplankton to survive. The krill in turn support baleen whales, manta rays, whale sharks, various seals, penguins, squid and fish. Krill is used as bait in sports fishing and the pharmaceutical industry. Krill oil is said to be a good source of the omega 3 oils DHA and EPA. Fish, courtesy of the krill, is important in the human diet. However, if anything breaks the food chain, life as we know it could be catastrophic.

The English poet John Donne wrote these profound words half a millennia ago: *"No man is an island entire of itself; every man is a piece of the continent, a part of the main...any man's death diminishes me, because I am involved in mankind. And therefore never send to know for whom the bell tolls; it tolls for thee."*

It appears that the ultimate task for the pilgrim treading the Healing Paths of the Radical Spiritualist is to become part of humanity, help people not only to heal themselves but also to spread the power of healing consciousness throughout the community and beyond.

The world is in dire need of healing. If you can support genuine programs to help combat starvation and sickness around the world, do it. If you cannot, do not feel guilty, that response and pity are faces of the False Self, they do not serve any useful purpose.

The quality here is Compassion. Compassion, unconditional love and healing go hand-in-hand. They are an alliance forged in cosmic steel. The healer who seeks and works with these qualities has no self-interest, coming either from the physical world or the Spirit World.

The healer channels healing from the Creator, and directs it to those in need, all living things, individual or world communities. The qualities of love and compassion and healing are revealed by positive deeds and the student, walking the healing paths strives to attain these qualities.

EXERCISE: DEVELOPING ENERGY

This can be done alone or with a group of like-minded spiritual people sitting in a circle, comfortably seated with feet on the ground..

Focus on your breathing and feel centered with your eyes closed. Start the HU mantra, with lips just a little apart so you can feel the air passing through. Allow yourself to chant the HU...as in hoooooooo. Do this for several minutes.

Stop the chanting and rest for a minute or so. Then bring your hands close together but not touching and feel the energy. It will feel like a growing cushion of air. Slowly draw your hands apart until they are several inches apart. Now, slowly come back to the starting position, and again draw them apart until the gap is about four to six inches. Keep doing this action, drawing the palms further apart until they are some eight or nine inches apart.

Slowly bring your hands together, you will feel a cushion of energy existing between your hands, an invisible ball. Check it for resistance and elasticity. This gives you a sense of the bio-energetic field. You may also generate the same energy by attuning to Spirit and asking that you be a channel for healing energy.

Once the circle members feel the energy in their hands, each member turns their palms into the circle and send it out to either a specific person, a specific community (like the Haitians) or to *all those people who need healing now.* You may notice the pranic force increasing in your hands and flowing into the circle and out to the world.

Also, do not forget the creatures that God created to accompany us on our human journey. *"We send healing to all those animals that are suffering today."*

Perhaps Mr. Donne should have written "Because I am involved in Life."

KEEP HEALING TOPICAL

Resolve to have a healing circle every week, at your church, your spiritual center or even in your home. . Start it with a discussion of something you have read or heard on the news where people are suffering. This gives the circle topicality. Resist falling into the "pity" trap, weeping or sentimental displays. One other thing, keep a record. A diary or a journal is very useful for keeping track of members attending and healing sent out to the world.

If you find that you cannot get a healing circle operating, simply sit in a quiet place, indoors or outdoors and meditate, attune to the Cosmos for pranic energy, then send it out to people and animals that need healing. This will expand your consciousness, and as it happens, he or she who sends out healing, receives healing. It is the Universal Law of Giving.

LOVE YOURSELF ALWAYS

To be a healer, whether it is for others or yourself, it is important to love yourself. Much can be done in maintaining a healthy body simply by loving yourself. As I wrote in *Cracking the Glass Darkly*: *"Whatever you do in your life, love yourself for doing it and you will always do the right thing."*

Always remember, no matter who you are, whatever you are doing right now, YOU are a unique human being. There is only one you. You may look or sound like many others, but there is only one you. You are a special person. All of the information that your subconscious mind has collected makes you a unique person, a unique spiritual traveler, and, among all life on Planet Earth, human beings are the only life form that can consciously give healing to themselves and others.

And vitally important, as you go about your daily life work towards soul/spirit consciousness and seek the Sacred Sound of the Audible Sound Stream. This does not mean that you have to live in a secluded mountain-top retreat in the Andes. You can live it up and enjoy yourself at home, work or play and still be life conscious.

If you ever think that God, the Universal Mind, Infinite Intelligence, the Shabd, wanted you to live on Planet Earth and suffer, think again. People have been taught to suffer by so-called "holy men" who wish to manipulate and control. That is criminal nonsense. The challenge is to break free from the shackles of pain and suffering and heal by living in the Here and Now. It is vitally important. Gautama Buddha said it so well: *"The secret of health for both mind and body is not to mourn for the past, not to worry about the future, and not to anticipate troubles, but to live the present moment wisely and earnestly."*

Remember, there is no other time than right now. It is living in the Here and Now, meditating and healing in the present, that ultimately allows you to go deep down into your heart and find the stillness that exists in yourself and in each and everyone on the planet. When you find the stillness, you are healed. When you recognize that stillness, you are with the Creator, and it is in the stillness that you will hear and enjoy the sacred healing sounds of the Audible Life Stream, the Shabd,

This has been the teachings of all the great teachers. This has been the teachings and the Insights as we walked the various Healing Paths of the Radical Spiritualist. Go forth and heal.

Blessings! Robert

BOOKS AND CONNECTIONS FOR STUDY

BOOKS AND INFORMATION LINKS FOR STUDY ALONG THE HEALING PATHS.

RELAXATION AND IMAGERY

The Wizard Within by A. M. Krasner (Clinical Hypnotherapy)

The Science of Breath by Yogi Ramacharaka

The Self-Talk Solution by Shad Helmstetter

Self Mastery Through Conscious Autosuggestion by Emile Coué

HANDS ON AND SPIRIT HEALING

Spirit Healing by Harry Edwards

Therapeutic Touch: Inner Workbook by Dolores Kreiger

Accepting Your Power to Heal, by Dolores Krieger

Healing Touch: The Church's Forgotten Language by Zach Thomas

LIVING IN THE HERE AND NOW

The Power of the Supermind by Vernon Howard

The Mystic Path to Cosmic Power by Vernon Howard

Total Freedom by J. Krishnamurti

The Book of Life – Meditations by J. Krishnamurti

Cracking the Glass Darkly by Robert Egby

DOWSING AND DIVINING

Earth Radiation by Kathe Bachler & John Living

Pendulum Power by Greg Neilsen

Healing Sick Houses, Dowsing for Healthy Homes, by Roy and Ann Proctor

The Diviner's Handbook by Tom Graves

Acquavideo, an instruction guide by Bill Cox

Dowsing for Health by Arthur Bailey

American Society of Dowsers, The Water Dowsers Manual, compiled by Maria Perry

SOUND HEALING AND COLORS

Toning, the Creative Power of the Voice by Laurel Elizabeth Keyes

Sound Medicine by Wayne Perry

Toning, the Creative Power of the Voice by Laurel Elizabeth Keyes

Music and Sound in the Healing Arts, by John Beaulieu

Healing Sounds: The Power of Harmonics by Jonathan Goldman

MYSTICISM, SPIRITUALISM AND HIGHER AWARENESS

River of Life: How to Live in The Flow by Marilyn Awtry-Smith

The Ego: From Birth to Rebirth (Volume Six) by Paul Brunton

The Body (Volume Four, Part 2) Notebooks of Paul Brunton

The Ego: From Birth to Rebirth by Paul Brunton

Reincarnation by Joseph Head and S.L. Cranston

The Case for Reincarnation by Joe Fisher

Induced After Death Communication by Allan L. Botkin & R. Craig Hogan

The Scole Experiment by Grant and Jane Solomon

Witnessing the Impossible by Robin P. Foy

The Spiritualist Manual by the National Spiritualist Association of Churches

The Path of the Masters by Julian P. Johnson

History of Chinese Literature by Herbert A. Giles

Halley's Bible Handbook by Henry H. Halley

The Holy Bible

Man and His Gods by Homer W. Smith

The Spirits' Book by Allan Kardec

The Secret Life of Water by Masaru Emoto

Journeys Out of the Body by Robert Monroe

On Death and Dying by Elisabeth Kübler-Ross

The Mysticism of Sound and Music by Hazrat Inayat Khan

The Quest of the Radical Spiritualist by Robert Egby

Cracking the Glass Darkly by Robert Egby

SOURCES THAT MAY BE OF HELP

USA Spiritualist Churches Directory: www.nsac.org

Worldwide Directory Spiritualist Churches: www.lighthousespiritualcentre.ca/

British Spiritualist National Union: www.snu.org.uk/

National Guild of Hypnotists: www.ngh.net/

Sound Healers Association: www.soundhealersassociation.org/

The Mayo Clinic on stress: www.mayoclinic.com

Mental Health America: www.mentalhealthamerica.net

Peaceful Mind / Color Pinspot Lamp with colored lenses:
www.peacefulmind.com

American Society of Dowsers: www.dowsers.org

Aura House Courses for Color Therapy Practitioners:
www.aurahouse.com

Spectrahue Light & Sound Inc. Toronto, Canada: www.spectrahue.com

Native American Arts and Crafts: www.native-languages.org/flutes.htm

Odell Borg, Native American Flutes: www.highspirits.com

Robert Egby's Center for Hypnosis & Sound Healing: www.robert-egby.com

AUDIO CD PROGRAMS FOR NEW INSIGHTS
By Robert Egby

CD 103 -- ENHANCE YOUR PSYCHIC ABILITIES! Three programs designed for psychics and mediums who want to increase their psychic energy and build self-confidence in using their gifts for reading energy and relaying messages from loved ones and others in Spirit.

CD 104 -- SPIRIT GUIDES AND AURAS Two meditations -- both for Psychic Training. (1) "Meeting and Working with Spirit Guides" (2) "How to See Auras," a psychic imagery training program for seeing auras around all living things.

CD 105 -- THE POWER OF SELF HEALING! Two meditations using the power of imagery for self-healing. "The Garden of Harmony" and "A Child of the Sun." These meditations should not be used in place of professional medical care, but as a support for accelerated healing.

CD-107 -- SPIRIT RENDEZVOUS! Be Your Own Medium! Three unusual programs on Spirit Communication. (1) A talk on Spirit contact and the Spirit World and instructions for conducting the following meditation. (2) A Meditation for Meeting a Loved One or Friends in the Spirit World. (3) The Gatekeeper, a guide who takes you to meet ascended beings or whoever you pray to.

CD-111 -- JOURNEY TO LOVING YOURSELF A special self-empowerment program. Throughout the ages the great teachers have told us to "Love Yourself," but legacies have left us with imaginary and pointless limitations. In this program Robert Egby describes the physical, mental and spiritual benefits that come when we let go of limitations and link ourselves with the powerful universal love force -- which is our natural heritage. The CD presents a newly recorded beautiful and memorable meditation. This is one of two CD programs mentioned in Robert's book, "Cracking the Glass Darkly." The other is CD--112.

CD 112 -- THE DA VINCI MEDITATION Leonardo da Vinci the 15th century painter, inventor and philosopher was well aware of higher mystical teachings, particularly the phenomena of Living in the Here and Now. He gave an example in his famous "Notebooks" of how to live in the "Now". Robert has written and recorded a meditation based on this example. The CD presents three tracks: Robert discusses the elements of ancient teachings in "A New Way of Living" followed by "The da Vinci" meditation based on Leonardo's river observations. The CD contains a second meditation: "The Seven Pearls" which highlights the teachings of mystical thinking.

Please visit our website: www.robert-egby.com

ABOUT THE AUTHOR

 Robert Egby has been a teacher of self-empowerment, spiritual development and mysticism for over thirty years. His style is informative, personal, sometimes dramatic, sometimes humorous, but always ready to help anyone on the Quest for the True Self, the Universal Mind and Healing the Spirit.

Robert has passed through many doors in his own quest. Accredited war correspondent, award winning news photographer and broadcaster, public relations director, hypnoanalyst, dowser, sound healer, medium, and ordained minister. He has written and produced dozens of audio meditation and self-hypnosis programs, and this is his third book. The first was "Cracking the Glass Darkly" published in December 2007 and the second published in 2009 was "The Quest of the Radical Spiritualist: The Journey Home." This was a Finalist in the USA Book News National Best Books Awards 2009.

Robert lives with his partner, Betty Lou on Chaumont Bay, Lake Ontario where they conduct metaphysical and spiritual workshops and hold weekly development classes.

CPSIA information can be obtained at www.ICGtesting.com
Printed in the USA
BVOW041035250213

314028BV00003B/7/P